Parenting on the Autism Spectrum

A SURVIVAL GUIDE

Parenting on the Autism Spectrum

A SURVIVAL GUIDE

Lynn Adams, Ph.D., CCC-SLP
Autism Education Specialist

PLURAL
PUBLISHING
— INC. —
SAN DIEGO
OXFORD
BRISBANE

5521 Ruffin Road
San Diego, CA 92123

e-mail: info@pluralpublishing.com
Web site: http://www.pluralpublishing.com

49 Bath Street
Abingdon, Oxfordshire OX14 1EA
United Kingdom

FSC
Mixed Sources
Product group from well-managed
forests and other controlled sources

Cert no. SW-COC-002283
www.fsc.org
© 1996 Forest Stewardship Council

Typeset in 11/13 Garamond by Flanagan's Publishing Services, Inc.
Printed in the United States of America by McNaughton and Gunn

Library of Congress Cataloging-in-Publication Data

Adams, Lynn W.
    Parenting on the autism spectrum : a survival guide / Lynn Adams.
        p. cm.
    Includes bibliographical references and index.
    ISBN-13: 978-1-59756-289-8 (alk. paper)
    ISBN-10: 1-59756-289-0 (alk. paper)
    1. Autistic children—Care. 2. Parents of autistic children. I. Title.
    RJ506.A9A335 2009
    618.92'85882—dc22

                                              2009002735

Contents

Preface

I got this E-mail from a friend who is married to a man with characteristics of Asperger syndrome (AS), has a son diagnosed with AS, a daughter with high-functioning autism, and who recently took in a nephew with AS.

Lynn,

Thought you might get a kick out of what transpired at my house last night. Well, my 81-year-old grandpa came by last night and bought me a bucket full of grapes. Well, you know all people of that generation think all of the summer bounty needs to be preserved in a jar of some sort. He says "Here Kristal, I brought you some grapes so you can make some jelly." Thrilled as I am I say, "Wow, thanks Papa! I know what I will be doing tomorrow." You know me . . . diabetic . . . can't eat jelly. So here is where it gets comical with the whole autism twist . . . so many diverse reactions.

Husband Brian—"MMMM Jelly, you haven't made jelly since the summer you broke your leg."

Son Zachary—"JELLY?? I like jelly . . . can you make cherry jelly instead? I like cherry jelly. Do we have any cherry jelly here right now? (last seen going toward house . . . in search of cherry jelly).

Nephew Matthew—"JELLY!!!!! YOU KNOW HOW TO MAKE JELLY?!?!?!?! WOW THAT IS AWESOME! I can't wait to taste it. (Always nice to impress a teenager.) I just love jelly on toast, do I have to eat it hot? (Did I mention he won't eat or touch anything hot?)

Daughter Karie—"JELLY, I HATE JELLY!!! (covers mouth) I won't eat it. You won't make me eat it, will you Mommy?"

So here I am making jelly. I must admit the kitchen smells really good, but I am glad I am the only one here because I would probably be getting comments about the smell. I know you might not get the kick out of the whole thing like I did . . . but daily life here just gets more and more interesting.

Kristal

If I were a really talented writer I could have created that story, but real life is just so much better! I wrote this book at the urging of the many parents I have encountered over the years. Many said they wanted a book that would help them be proactive, not just reactive. I have endeavored to do that here. I hope that you find this a true guide for surviving the adventure you will embark on as you raise your child with an autism spectrum disorder.

Thanks to all the families I have worked with, met, loved, laughed, and cried with over the past 20 years. This book is for you.

Dedication

This volume is dedicated to the Edwards Family.

To Kristal, who is a tower of strength and incredibly funny.

To Brian, who was smart enough to marry Kristal.

To Zachary, the future chef, and Karie, the girl with the biggest heart in the world!

CHAPTER 1

Parenting 101

❖ Truths ❖

Parenting is one of the hardest jobs one can undertake. Having a child diagnosed with an autism spectrum disorder (ASD) takes parenting to a whole other level. The challenges parents face are many and the solutions may seem to be few and far between. Understanding the nature of the disorders found on the autism spectrum is the first step to being empowered as a parent. The old adage "knowledge is power" is an old adage because it is true.

The first truth parents must embrace is that having an autism spectrum disorder is an explanation for behavior and differences, but it should never be used as an excuse. Parents may want to excuse problem behavior or challenges related to ASD, but this will not facilitate their success in preparing their child for the biggest hurdle—living in the real world. It is incumbent on parents and professionals to prepare children with ASD to live their fullest lives, with as much independence and success as possible.

The second truth is that embracing the first truth will be hard. There will be times when it will seem easier to just make an excuse for the child, when it will be easier to say "He can't help it, he has autism." What is true is that he has autism. What is not true is the idea that the child cannot "help" but engage in a certain behavior. We must help him engage in the most productive and meaningful behaviors as much as humanly possible.

Other truths include the following:

❖ Every child with ASD is unique, with his or her own set of skills, strengths, and needs.

❖ There is no one method of treatment or intervention that can cure or "fix" the ASD.

❖ There is a lot of information on ASD available to parents, but just because it is published, does not make that information valid, meaningful, or appropriate (Willis, 2006).

❖ Myths ❖

Mythology surrounding autism spectrum disorders abounds. Common myths include the following:

❖ Children with ASD live in their own little world and cannot break out of it.

❖ Children with ASD do not want to socialize with other persons.

❖ Children with ASD are not able to express emotions.

❖ Children with ASD do not like to be touched or hugged.

❖ Children with ASD all have special skills or talents.

❖ Children with ASD are all mentally challenged.

❖ Children with ASD cannot learn to communicate or interact with others.

❖ Children with ASD cannot learn . . . period.

None of these points are accurate or born out by the literature. Children with ASD can learn, can communicate, can interact, and can indeed break out of their "world" (Aspy & Grossman, 2007; Willis, 2006).

❖ Definitions ❖

In the 1940s, two men, an ocean apart, began describing unusual social communication behaviors being observed in children. Independently, each physician began to identify subtypes that now fall under the umbrella of autism spectrum disorders. Although the two men were contemporaries, they never collaborated but interestingly produced strikingly similar papers which continue to serve as seminal works.

Autism

Kanner (1943) described children who were socially aloof, demonstrated language deficits, a need for sameness, and a significant need to be left alone. The current diagnostic criterion for autism includes deficits in social skills, restricted patterns of behavior, and communication concerns. Social skill needs can include poor eye contact, difficulty with personal space maintenance, and a lack of social reciprocity. The restricted patterns of behavior may involve repetitive actions, and stereotypical movements. Communication concerns can range from muteness to very mild language deficits. Associated features, those not required for diagnosis but co-occurring with autism , are sensory differences (unusual responses to sounds, pain, taste, smells, light, touch, movement); cognitive differences (poor organizational skills, problems with generalization of learning from context to context); and motor differences (balance concerns, poor eye hand coordination) (Aspy & Grossman, 2007).

Asperger Syndrome

In Eastern Europe in 1944, Hans Asperger described a disorder similar to that presented by Kanner. He noted children who demonstrated social communication deficits that took the form of pedantic conversational skills. These children tended to lecture others on topics of their choosing rather than engaging in the typical give and take of conversations. Asperger noted that the children he encountered also demonstrated normal cognitive functioning, and had no delay in general language acquisition. The reason Asperger syndrome seems like a new disorder, even though Asperger was a contemporary of Kanner, is that Asperger wrote his paper in 1944 during World War II, and it was not translated into English until 1981 (Ozonoff, Dawson, & McPartland, 2002).

Asperger Syndrome and High Functioning Autism

Although Asperger defined only the syndrome that bears his name, it is noted that children with high functioning autism (HFA) have a great deal in common with those with Asperger syndrome (AS). Children with AS and HFA present with social differences such as mindblindness (difficulty recognizing feelings or thoughts of others), lack of tact, difficulty making and maintaining friendships, naiveté often leading to bullying, problems with body language, and comprehension of jokes. Behavioral concerns include a need for sameness, eccentricity, and difficulty transitioning between activities or events. With regard to communication, differences noted include immediate and delayed echolalia, literal interpretation of figurative language, difficulty engaging in conversation, difficulty asking for help, making irrelevant comments, excessive talking, use of an advanced vocabulary, and difficulty talking about the interests of others (Aspy & Grossman, 2007).

Additionally, children with HFA/AS experience sensory challenges (unusual reactions to input any/all senses, humming or singing), cognitive differences which can include, but are not limited to, narrow interests, complex internal fantasy worlds, and extensive factual knowledge with limited abstract reasoning. Children with HFA/AS often are described as having motor deficits that can involve clumsiness, awkward gait, executive function deficits (starting and/or completing tasks), poor handwriting, and refusal to complete handwriting tasks. Of particular interest are the emotional challenges experienced by children with HFA/AS. Children with HFA/AS often experience significant anxiety and stress. They seem to have a low tolerance for frustration and may turn that frustration inward in self-injury or outward in a meltdown (Aspy & Grossman, 2007).

❖ Theories Related to ASD, Its Causes, ❖ and Characteristics

Causes

Genetic/Chromosomal Factors

Because ASD tends to run in families, there appears to be an underlying genetic component. Additionally, twin studies have demonstrated that, if one identical twin has autism, the other will have a 60% chance of being impacted as well (Ozonoff, Dawson, & McPartland, 2002). Recent studies have pointed to some genes putting some children at risk for the development of an ASD (Volkmar, Westphal, Gupta, & Wiesner, 2008). Over 100 different genes have been examined for a relationship to the development of ASD (Wassnik, Brzustowicz, Bartlett, & Szmatmari, 2004). In the last few years, studies have pointed to a few specific genes as being related to the development of ASD. Both the EN2 (Benayed et al., 2005) and the MET (Campbell et al., 2006) genes have been shown to be associated with ASD. Several other rare genetic mutations have been noted in other genes (Durrand et al., 2007; Sutcliffe et al., 2005). However, there have been no studies to show a single gene might be the culprit. That makes treatment from a genetic standpoint extremely challenging. Some chromosomal anomalies have been found to result in characteristics of ASD such as 18q deletion syndrome and fragile X syndrome (Rutter, 2000).

Infections

Viral infections occurring both before and after delivery have the potential to result in ASD. These can include, but are not limited to, encephalitis, cytomegalovirus, herpes simplex virus, and congenital rubella (Bach, 2005; Janzen, 2003; Sweeten, Posey, & McDougle, 2004). Studies have shown that children with ASD have more ear infections, allergies, pediatrician visits, and hospitalizations relative to those in control groups (Croen, Najjar, Ray, Lotspeich, & Bernal, 2006; Jepson, 2007; Neihus & Lord, 2006). As viruses can mutate and evolve with apparent ease, prevention of ASD and other central nervous system disorders caused by viral infection will continue to be problematic.

Metabolic Challenges

Jepson (2007) refers to autism as a multisystem metabolic disease, not simply a neurologic disorder. Jepson states that it is the interactions among the brain, gut, and immune system, each susceptible to damage from toxins, oxidative stress, and inflammation, that lend credence to this perspective. Metabolic concerns include false neurotransmitters or neurotoxins which result in diet-derived peptides (opiatelike substances from wheat and milk proteins), and gut dysbiosis (abnormal pathogens in the bowel that affect the brain). Additionally, the modulation of neurotransmitters falls under this heading and dietary issues apparently can result in changes in the function of neurotransmitters (Jepson, 2007).

Environmental Toxins/Chemicals

In his 2007 text, *Changing the Course of Autism*, Jepson discusses, at length, the potential relationship between environmental toxins and autism. He refers specifically to the gut issues of children with ASD. He references the work of Andrew Wakefield and his characterization of "autistic enterocolitis." Dr. Jill James, a biochemist, noted abnormal transmethylation and transsulfuration. Both processes relate to the methylation cycle, which is critical to detoxification and antioxidation in the human body. The reader is encouraged to read Dr. Jepson's seminal text for more information on the relationship of the environment and autism.

❖ Characteristics ❖

Executive Function

Executive function is defined as the ability to plan, organize, and complete tasks as well as multitasking. It requires a great number of mental or cognitive processes including memory, behavior inhibition, mental flexibility, performance monitoring, and self-regulation (Aspy & Grossman, 2007). The literature suggests that executive function deficits are noted in persons with ASD; however, the current literature does not support the premise that these deficits are at the core of ASD or merely a concomitant symptom (Hughes, 2001). The frontal lobes of the brain (think forehead) appear to be the controlling structures for these types of skills and activities (Goldberg, 2001).

Theory of Mind

The ability to take another's perspective and to recognize how our actions impact others is central to social cognition or theory of mind (ToM). Whether a deficit in ToM is central to ASD has not been determined, but certainly, this cognitive skill is important in the successful navigation of the social world (Baron-Cohen, Tager-Flusberg, & Cohen, 1993). Problems with ToM can result in what is referred to as "mindblindness." Mindblindness can limit a person's ability to understand, explain, and predict the behaviors of other people. Many have seen a child accidentally bump into a child with ASD only to the have the child with ASD claim that they were hit. Mindblindness impacts the child's ability to judge what is accidental and what is intentional (Baron-Cohen & Swettenham, 1997).

Central Coherence

The integration of information into a cogent and meaningful whole is the thrust of central coherence. Frith (1989) presented an explanation of the cognitive challenges seen in children with ASD as being secondary to a problem with central coherence. This perspective has received support in the exiting literature (Booth, Charlton, Hughes, & Happe, 2003; Burnette et al., 2005; Pellicano, Maybery, & Durkin, 2005). It is most likely that an interplay of all three, executive function, ToM, and weak central coherence is at work in most children on the autism spectrum.

❖ Challenges for Parents ❖

Behavior, both good and bad, must be noted, interpreted, and addressed by the parents. Consistency of response will be the key to success in this area. Chapter 2 provides information regarding the nature of problem behavior, the need for a behavior plan, and the importance of choice making skills.

The physical space in which the family lives and functions will have an impact on the development of the child with ASD. Chapter 3 focuses on the importance of home organization, dietary challenges, sensory needs, and more.

From the moment a child is diagnosed until the day he or she leaves the planet, that child needs a schedule. The importance of schedules are presented in Chapter 4 with information on the creation and use of daily, monthly, and minischedules.

Academics—the word alone can spike fear in the hearts of parents. This need not be the case. Chapter 5 contains information on supporting the child in school. Additionally, the challenge of the hidden curriculum is discussed.

Great attention and emphasis is placed on the development of play and social skills. Because play is a prerequisite for social skill acquisition, the focus of Chapter 6 is on the normal development of play, effective interventions and pitfalls to avoid.

Finally, Chapter 7 provides insights gained from real parents, for real parents.

The reader will find that I give my beliefs, based on the last 20 years of working with children on the spectrum in each chapter. This is not meant to show favoritism to any theory, approach, strategy, therapy, or intervention. It is to provide you with whatever benefit that might be gained from my experience.

CHAPTER 2

Managing Behavior
Before It Manages You

Perhaps the greatest challenges a parent of a child with ASD faces are behavior challenges. Most importantly, it is vital to remember that behavior can be both good and bad. We tend to focus on the bad stuff and forget to recognize the good things that children accomplish. Problem behavior can result from a number of causes: communication deficits, stress and fatigue, and inconsistent expectations, to name a few. Behaviors can be described as problematic when they fall into five categories: dangerous, destructive, disruptive, disgusting, and developmentally inappropriate (Hieneman, Childs, & Sergay, 2006).

❖ Addressing Communication Needs ❖

The most important lesson I have learned over the years is that *behaviors are messages*. This means problem behaviors are messages, not isolated incidents to be punished. Behavior does not occur in a vacuum. Something triggers it. Something serves as the antecedent. This antecedent should be identified so that it can either be avoided in the future or that an alternative response can be developed. Parents are the experts when it comes to observing and noting their child's problem behaviors. Parents spend the largest block of time with the child in the widest array of settings. Parents have greater opportunity to determine antecedents to problem behavior than most other adults it the child's life. Other than time spent attending school, the child is usually in the company of one of his parents.

Once a problem behavior occurs, it is imperative that the parents begin observing to determine the antecedent. The focus at this point is on the trigger for the behavior and not on the consequence. With any luck at all, we will find out what triggers the behavior and avoid that in the future. If the trigger cannot be avoided (nap time), then we can help the child cope by giving him or her alternative behaviors. We can set up a schedule for nap time so that the child knows how long he or she will be napping, and what desired activity will follow the nap. Some children scream to make a request, we can replace that problem behavior with words, gestures. or pictures.

A review of the literature shows that problem behaviors can be significantly decreased when communication skills are increased (Charlop-Christy, Carpenter, Le Blanc, & Kellet, 2002; Janzen, 2003;

Koegel & Koegel, 2006; Magiati & Howlin, 2003; Sherer & Schreibman, 2005). Therefore, the first task at hand following diagnosis is the development of a functional communication system. For some children with ASD, this will be a picture-based system whereas others will rely on oral language for communicative purposes. Regardless of the modality, a child who can communicate is less likely to have to rely on problem behaviors to get his needs met (Klinger & Dawson, 1992).

Intervention Strategies

Communication intervention strategies have been shown to increase effective communication and decrease problem behavior.

PECS

The Picture Exchange Communication System (PECS) uses pictures to augment and facilitate the development of functional communication skills. When a child can ask for a cookie and receive the same by exchanging a picture, there is little need for screaming or yelling (Charlop-Christy et al., 2002; Magiati & Howlin, 2003). PECS is the best known, systematized picture communication approach. Through discrete trial training, the child learns to associate pictures with desired objects and events. The procedure for training on a PECS system is clearly outlined and specific in materials produced by the authors. To summarize, the child is presented with a picture paired with a desired object. Using hand-over-hand assistance, if necessary, the child is assisted in giving the picture to the communication partner in order to obtain the desired item. As soon as possible. the amount of cuing and prompting is reduced so that the child is able to independently bring a picture to receive an item. Once this basic skill has been established, more pictures are added. Once proficiency is attained, carrier phrases can be added to include statements such as "I see a _____." A limitation of PECS comes from the need for two adults to fully participate in the training period. It is often challenging to find two adults available at the same time. Another concern arises from the fact that the discrimination phase of the process comes after substantial training has occurred on only one picture. In my experience, some children do not realize that the picture is actually a symbol for a specific item, and may just learn to give any picture to receive the desired item. The authors stated in a training session that one can certainly alter the procedure, but that it should not be called PECS if altered. I encourage the use of a blank card paired with the picture of the desired item from the beginning. This ensures that the child knows from the start that the picture means the thing. If the child ever gives the blank card, the trainer should realize that the symbolic association has not been made.

PRT

Another effective treatment approach is Pivotal Response Training (PRT). PRT improves communication by focusing on motivation, multiple cues, self-initiation, and self-management. The improvement in verbal communication reduces the need for nontraditional communication (Koegel & Koegel, 2006). PRT is a combination of discrete trial principles and those of naturalistic, incidental teaching. The primary focus of PRT is to maximize motivation. PRT includes offering choices, and making treatment targets functional for the individual child. There are a number of effective treatments for communication treatment. Once a treatment is chosen, it is absolutely essential that this treatment approach be used in the home and all environments. It cannot be a school-only treatment. It does not work that way. Parents must dedicate time to the practice of the communication treatment strategies. Nothing is more disheartening than to have a child make progress in a treatment environment, but not have that treatment carried over in the home and community. For the professional who sees that something works but is not being practiced, frustration can set it. This is not an indictment of parents. Parents may be intimidated by the idea of practicing the strategy. If that is the case, parents must ask for training, support, help, whatever is needed to alleviate fears and allow practice.

Providing Choices

Studies also have demonstrated that offering choices to children with ASD can decrease problem behaviors (Dunlap et al., 1994);

Foster-Johnson, Ferro, & Dunlap, 1994). Instead of asking the child what she wants to wear, offer her a choice of two outfits that she enjoys wearing. The ability to control some aspects of one's life can decrease problem behavior while increasing independence. Dunlap et al (1994) studied the relationship between choosing between two tasks, versus having no choice in task selection. They found that the choice-making condition was superior to the other condition with regard to task engagement. Additionally, disruptive behavior decreased in the choice-making condition. In a similar vein, Foster-Johnson, Ferro, and Dunlap (1994) found that participation in preferred curricular activities reduced problem behavior and increased desirable behavior.

A meta-analysis of the literature published from 1996 to 2000 showed the following trends relative to behavior intervention: (a) stereotypical behaviors are studied most often; (b) a wide range of interventions have been studied; (c) behavioral interventions are effective; (d) a diagnosis of autism did not affect the likelihood of intervention success; (e) functional assessment increases the intervention success; (f) familiar adults using interventions increased the positive effect of the intervention; and (g) changes in the environment increase intervention effectiveness (Horner, Carr, Strain, Todd, & Reed, 2002). These findings tell us that we need to pay attention to behavior and what it means. They tell us that parents are vital to the success of behavior intervention and that practicing behavior changes in a variety of settings increases the benefits of intervention.

Key to any successful behavior intervention program is an analysis of the function of the behavior. A functional behavioral assessment identifies the relationship between the behavior itself, the environment, and the learner. Once a behavior has been identified and its function or purpose determined, a comprehensive plan can be developed to deal with the problem behavior, usually by increasing skills and abilities. Functional behavior analysis is different from more traditional behavior modification techniques. Traditional approaches focus on the consequence of a problem behavior, not why the behavior occurred in the first place. Although the traditional behavior modification approach is useful for children who do not have ASD, it does not serve those with ASD nearly as well. When one focuses on punishing problem behavior without replacing the behavior with a more functional skill, the problem behavior may morph into a different form. For example, if the child with ASD bites when asked to stop playing and we punish the biting, he may stop biting, but he still does not have a functional way to express his being upset. He may stop biting and begin hitting instead. We need to help him develop an acceptable alternative behavior to replace the biting. See Janzen (2003) for an excellent discussion of the process for assessing and developing behavior plans. Numerous worksheets and forms are provided to facilitate the successful assessment.

Parents may find themselves most comfortable in providing rewards and punishment. Once a behavioral plan has been developed, the parent will likely be in control of the activities/items that reinforce acceptable and compliant behavior. For an activity/item to continue to be rewarding, the child cannot have free access to it. If the child can play a favorite video game without time limitations, the game will not serve as the powerful reinforcer it could be if access was restricted. Parents have to be willing to control access to highly motivating and desired activities. Children with ASD often demonstrate limited interest and attention to many typical play activities. Once you find something the child loves, you have to control access to it or the child may satiate. Satiation means the child can get so much of the favorite activity that he or she no longer wants it. Then, it has lost its value as a reinforcer. If you have every eaten too much of a favorite food, to the point of feeling sick, you know that is usually a long time before you want to eat that food again. This is satiation.

Generally, the focus of most behavior intervention programs is on the aberrant behavior. It is also very important for parents to catch their child with ASD being good. It is vital that children learn when they are on the right track. A study of the language used in professional, working class, and poor homes showed that the children in the professional families heard positive affirmations (Good job!) more that twice as often as they heard prohibitions (Stop that!). In the poor families, the prohibitions outnumbered the positive statements by more than 2 to 1 (Hart & Risly, 1995). The importance of rewarding the good stuff, as well as dealing with the bad stuff, cannot be overstated. What can happen is that we spend so much time and energy dealing with the bad behavior that we forget or do not have the enthusiasm to praise the good behavior. If we do not praise and reinforce when the child makes a good choice or demonstrates good behavior, how will the child know he is doing the right thing? Just as we focus on changing the undesirable behavior, we must focus on the good behaviors we see every day.

Rules rule! Children with ASD tend to respond well to rules and in fact are often very rule driven. It is imperative that the rules for behavior be discussed among all adults involved in the rearing and care of the child with ASD. Once the rules are agreed on, they need to be posted and reviewed daily, if not weekly. One cannot rely on the child to recall the rules independently. Additionally, rules apply outside of the home and should be written down and taken with the family. Parents should not underestimate the power of rules in managing behavior. Knowing the rules beforehand can keep problems from occurring.

❖ An Ounce of Prevention ❖

Three strategies can be used to avoid problem behaviors altogether. The first strategy is to steer clear of situations that are known to cause problem behavior. If one knows that a person, place, or thing can prompt a behavioral issue, one can just avoid the same. By the same token, if one knows their child will be more likely to have a problem in a situation (e.g., the child is overly tired or sick), one should not place the child in that situation if at all possible. However, constantly shielding the child from the challenging situation does not allow the child to grow, develop and adapt (Hieneman, Childs, & Sergay, 2006). Planning ahead can allow parents to avoid problems altogether. Sometimes it can be as simple as packing lunch, and setting out the breakfast dishes and clothing the night before a school day. This alleviates stress on the part of the parent and the child. Alleviating stress can alleviate problem behaviors. Not having to rush around in the morning, scrambling to get a lunch together, and choosing a shirt can make all the difference in the tone of the day.

The second strategy is to be used when the trigger situation cannot be avoided. The parent can follow the undesired activity with a preferred activity. This is the application of the "first, then" technique. First, we will do something you do not enjoy, and then we will do something you do enjoy. It is essential that the communication between the child and parent be clear and direct. Adults often ask questions when they mean to give directions. For example, asking the child, "Can you please sit down?" may elicit a yes/no response when that was *not* the intent of the message. Avoid asking questions when you are giving directions. Being clear and direct will decrease the chance of miscommunications, and, hopefully, decrease the occurrence of undesirable behavior. Choice making is also a part of this strategy, allowing the child to begin to develop independence and effective decision-making skills. If the child is facing several chores, allow the child to choose which task to complete first (Hieneman, Childs, & Sergay, 2006).

Finally, the parent can help bring about positive behavior by adding cues that support and prompt the desired behavior. If the parent explains what is expected with regard to behavior in a certain situation, he or she increases the likelihood that the child will navigate that situation successfully. For example, Mom has a list of errands to complete with the child in tow. The mother can prompt the child with her expectations. Prior to entering the grocery store, Mom can review the rules for the store. If the event is going to last longer than the child might be able to tolerate, cues noting how much longer shopping might take can help alleviate many problem behaviors (Hieneman, Childs, & Sergay, 2006).

❖ When the Fit Happens ❖

Most adults find a fit or meltdown most difficult to deal with, however it is important for parents to remember that fits happen because they work. The fit allows the child to avoid certain people, places, or things. If parents are not careful, the fit gets the child what he wants—a toy, a treat, whatever their heart desires. Once a fit has worked to the benefit of the child, it is likely to reoccur. Hieneman, Childs, and Sergay (2006) noted that the ultimate goal of behavior management is to help the child achieve his or her desired outcome through positive behavior, not problem behavior. They note that children often act out to gain attention. Parents must endeavor to have everyone who interacts with their child praise the good behavior while ignoring the bad (if possible). If the child seems to be behaving badly just for the sake of behaving badly, redirection is imperative. Find a physical activity or other outlet for the energy being put into the fit. When the child misbehaves in an attempt to gain a toy or other item, parents must make sure that those items are available only when the child behaves appropriately. The child's fit should never get the desired item as this just strengthens the value of the fit for the child. Sometimes, misbehavior occurs because the child is trying to avoid a task or situation. Although the task cannot be avoided forever, the parent may find that by adjusting the schedule or giving the child a break, the child can then complete the less desired task. It is vital, however, that the fit not result in the task being completely avoided. Get the fit under control and go back and complete the required task. If the child destroys a paper, hand him another. Remember the scene in *The Miracle Worker*, the story of Helen Keller and Annie Sullivan, where Annie teaches Helen to use a spoon. Annie puts a spoon in Helen's hand and Helen throws it. Annie hands her another spoon. Helen throws it. Annie has *lots* of spoons. Annie wins that battle. The point is you have to persevere, you have to remain calm; you, the parent, has to stick it out and win.

Janzen (2003) endorses a process for solving or preventing problem behaviors. The first step involves assessing the problem. The assessment should include identification of the causes of the problem. It cannot be stressed enough that one must attempt to determine the cause of the problem. Time spent focusing on the consequences of the problem generally does not diminish the behavior when it comes to ASD. Why doesn't this seem to work? It doesn't work because, until you determine the cause of the problem behavior, you cannot determine how and if you can change the behavior. Once the causes have been noted, the second step is to organize and structure the environment so that factors that contribute to the problem can be eliminated or diminished. This is the most challenging aspect of behavior management for most parents. Why? Because life happens! It is often unpredictable. The best laid plans can certainly fall apart through no fault of the parent or child. If you know what causes the problem, you can increase your chances of avoiding that trigger. But some triggers cannot be avoided. Step three focuses on the teaching of new skills, concepts, and rules when triggers cannot be avoided and a replacement behavior or skill is necessary. Finally, parents need to understand that they will have to continuously evaluate and refine the behavior intervention process as the needs of the child are always changing. These four steps can be used to address behavior ranging from toileting needs, picky eating, and sleep issues. Virtually any behavior can be addressed using this process. Parents will be relieved to note, however, that many books are available to deal with the myriad problem behaviors demonstrated by the child with ASD.

❖ Teenagers: A Breed Apart ❖

Teens on the autism spectrum bring a whole different set of challenges to the behavioral arena. In addition to the concerns that come with ASD, parents are now dealing with hormones. The emergence of hormones can impact behavior dramatically as anger may be added to the mix. Anger is certainly a typical human emotion, but its manifestation in the child with ASD may bring additional stress into an already emotionally charged situation. Kellner (2003) noted several guiding principles that apply when addressing anger concerns. They include:

1. Parents and caregivers are role models: If the parents and caregivers are demonstrating anger, they should expect a similar response from the child.

2. No two people are alike: Even though the parent and child are related, it is unlikely that what works for one will work for the other.

3. Adolescents are stuck between childhood and adulthood: That betwixt and between time is hard on all kids and especially those with ASD. As the child struggles to develop a sense of his or her evolving role, behaviors that had been extinguished may return. Additionally, many children with HFA and AS tend to view themselves as peers to adults, even in childhood. This can make the transition to "teenhood" more complicated.

4. Anger can work to your benefit, if you learn how to use it: If you learn to express anger in an appropriate way, you can get your needs met. It is okay to be angry, it is a real emotion. Used in a constructive way, we can reach our desired outcome.

5. Each parent has his or her own parenting style: Some parents
    like the give and take of a discussion when upset, others may
    find criticism or negativity from their teen inappropriate. It is
    vital, however, to engage in dialogue with teens in order to
    effectively deal with anger. Silence is not the choice in this
    situation, calm sharing is.

❖ What I Believe ❖

I believe that children on the spectrum are among the most difficult children to raise. The behavior challenges make this the hardest job many will ever encounter. However, *being on the autism
spectrum explains problem behavior, but it does not excuse it.*
Yes, he screams because he has autism, but he screams for a reason.
If you never find out the reason for the screaming, you are slapping
a Band-Aid on a hemorrhage and, well, you see where I am going.
If you do not determine *why* a behavior occurs, and *what* the
behavior means, you may succeed in eradicating one aberrant
behavior only to have it replaced by another aberrant behavior.
Find out what the message in the behavior is, then replace the
unwanted behavior with one that gets the needs met and is more
socially acceptable. You simply cannot throw up your hands and
say, "Oh, he has autism and he screams because he has autism." I
would submit that he screams because he has no alternative available to him. He is trying desperately to communicate his wants and
needs and he has no way to do that.

I believe that if you are as consistent as is humanly possible in
parenting your child with ASD, you will reap the benefits as your
child grows up. If you are clear and unequivocal in your messages
to your child, you will see your child develop the self-regulation
skills necessary to successfully navigate the future. Children with
ASD need to learn alternate behaviors and coping strategies. It is
not enough to tell the child to stop doing something without also
telling him what he should do instead.

If, however, you fear making your child cry, or if you are not
able to maintain a calm and assertive demeanor, you are likely to
see problem behaviors maintained and even expanded. Yes, you

may have to step over your crying child as you walk out of the room. Sometimes, you have to be willing to ignore his being upset. This is not a permanent condition and your child will not be irreparably harmed if you let him cry it out. Giving into a fit of crying or even screaming can be the only alternative, but it should be your last resort. Walk out of the store if the fit threatens. Leave the cart, tell the greeter, and leave the store. There is someone there whose job it is to restock the groceries. You will do your child a greater service by having clear expectations. You will do yourself a service.

If people stare at you when the fit happens, ask them if they know about autism spectrum disorders. Share awareness if you can and then go deal with the problem. The word "empowerment" became somewhat clichéd in the last century, but a successful parent is empowered by not being intimidated by the label of ASD. By sharing information with others, you build awareness that your child has been impacted by one of the most challenging disorders around. But, if you deal with problem behavior in a direct, head-on manner, both you, your child, and family will build a foundation for later learning.

Dr. John Rosemond (2008), a family psychologist, said in a recent column, "Do your child a favor—never tolerate tantrums." He stated with great eloquence and candor that there is a disturbing trend to "pathologize" tantrums in preschoolers and to address said "pathology" with psychotropic drugs. This is the disease model that many follow. Dr. Rosemond in a more practical twist suggested that tantrums after the third birthday say more about the parents than the child. He notes that, prior to the parenting shift of the 1960s and 1970s, tantrums after age three were rarely discussed in the literature. Dr. Rosemond suggests that we have made children into dictators by conceding to their tantrums. Frankly, there seems to be a great deal of truth in this. And this truth can easily be applied to children with ASD. If you give in to the tantrum, expect another tantrum when the situation occurs again. You teach children how to behave when you reinforce their behavior. When a child begs for a toy in the local supercenter and you say no over and over only to finally say yes, please do not be upset with your child when the begging begins before you even exit the car on the next trip to the store.

CHAPTER 3

Autism in the House

It might not seem important but the management of the house, and all that is in the house, can contribute to the success of the child with ASD. Children with ASD tend to be visual learners, so that an excess of visual clutter could cause undue stress and interfere with successful learning or task completion. An organized, streamlined home can lead to an organized child. A disorganized home can cause anxiety and upset that can be avoided. No one likes to run around in the morning looking for a missing shoe or homework paper. It can set a bad tone for the day.

❖ Whole House Organization ❖

All the rooms in the home need to be organized and structured so that the maximum in growth and development can occur for the child with ASD. Some children with ASD are on special diets that require organization in the kitchen. Some families install sensory equipment to aid in sensorimotor development for the child with ASD. Common living areas in the home need to be family friendly while also meeting the needs of the child with ASD. Finally, the bedroom of the child with ASD requires special attention to allow it to be a calming, nurturing space.

Childproofing

Childproofing the home is essential for the arrival of any child and is particularly important when a child with ASD is in the home (O'Brien & Daggett, 2006). Parents need to pay attention to doors and door locks. Placing safety latches or locks high on exterior doors is important. If the yard is not fenced, fence it and make sure that gates in the yard are locked as well. Make sure medications are safely locked up; especially children's vitamins as they can be tasty and easily consumed like candy. Fasten heavy furniture like bookshelves to the wall with safety strapping. Many children with ASD are climbers and unsecured furniture becomes highly dangerous for them. Some parents remove the knobs that operate the stove to prevent accidental activation. If you have pets, make sure their food dishes, litterboxes, and toys are out of the child's reach. Some with

ASD report that fluorescent lights can cause physical discomfort and trigger problem behavior. Although we are all trying to be greener in our daily lives, you may find that the compact fluorescent bulbs are not functional for your household.

Organization Tips

If you have the luxury of hiring a professional organizer to help you get the house in order, good for you. If you do not have the means to do this, take a few tips here. Most people with ASD tend to be more visual in their processing of information. By extraction, one may assume that storage should allow the person to see items while keeping them stored and organized. Many stores offer a variety of storage solutions that include sturdy but clear containers. Toys, clothes, school items, and the like can be stored in clear containers. By not relying on the hanging rod in a closet and investing a few dollars in shelving, a parent can make the most of a closet by allowing some hanging space with much more area devoted to containerized storage. Furthermore, having a finite area for storage in the child's room can help keep the number of toys purchased in check. You will see later in this chapter that I am not an advocate of more is better when it comes to toys.

❖ Order in the Kitchen ❖

Many children with ASD become described as picky eaters. They seem to prefer certain textures and types of food. According to Ernsperger and Stegen-Hanson (2004), children with ASD often travel beyond picky eating and become what they term "resistant" eaters. This would be considered the extreme end of the eating spectrum, where children have serious food aversions that significantly impact their ability to eat a healthy, balanced diet. The characteristics of a resistant eater include:

❖ Eating only 10 to 15 foods

❖ Eating from only some of the food groups

❖ Tantruming/gagging with the presentation of new foods

❖ Demanding foods be present at every meal and prepared in the same manner every time

❖ Diagnosis of ASD.

This list is striking in that includes the diagnosis of ASD as one of its criteria (Ernsperger & Stegen-Hanson, 2004). This should alert parents to the need to be ever vigilant with regard to their child's eating habits. All effort should be made to avoid the development of resistant eating. Along the same lines, children with specific food preferences must not be given free access to those foods. Once a child has satiated his or her hunger, the introduction of new and different foods is likely to be unsuccessful. Parents may find that they must lock up foods to control access. Some children with ASD refuse to eat foods that come in different packaging or presentation even though the foods are essentially identical. A parent with whom I worked lamented the fact that her local grocery store stopped carrying the brand of french fries her children preferred. I suggested she keep a package from the preferred brand and put the new brand in the old package. Additionally, she was encouraged to consider presenting the equivalent food without the preferred wrappings, and to ignore the protests. After a couple days, the transition was made as the desire for fries outweighed the desire for the known wrapper and they ate the new fries.

Factors that can contribute to the development of resistant eating vary from environmental issues to behavioral challenges. For some children with ASD, deficits in physical, sensory, and neurologic development can play into eating concerns. Ernsperger and Stegen-Hanson (2004) listed the most common factors that include food neophobia, environmental issues, cultural concerns, and developmental challenges.

Food neophobia is defined as the fear of new foods. Although this is a part of normal development in the neurotypical child at about two years of age, it can seriously impact the course of the development of eating habits if parents succumb to the instinct to remove the refused food. Most children outgrow this period of neophobia by age five, but if foods are refused and not reintroduced, the parent may unwittingly assist in the development of long-term food phobia. Parents must endeavor to continue to present foods that have been rejected in the past. Place the food in front of the child and ignore the child's response, whether that is to eat the food or reject it. If the parent responds to either eating or rejecting, the child may use this response to control the situation.

Family schedules and demands can make mealtime chaotic. Parents often find that their child is not hungry when mealtimes vary and may supplement the child during the day with what is commonly referred to as "grazing" (eating/snacking throughout the day). This certainly disrupts appetite and, when combined with the presentation of new foods, makes it unlikely that the child will be readily willing to try the new food. Parents often find their child is more willing to eat if placed in front of the television watching a preferred show. This may seem a rather innocuous strategy, but watching TV does not facilitate successful eating in the long term.

When parents make the child's eating the focus of attention, the child may recognize eating as a chance for control. Many parents find themselves begging and cajoling their child to eat. This may seem like a valid technique but, in fact, it places undue attention to eating that ultimately can make a resistant eater even more resistant. A strategy used with children who have behavior-based eating challenges (not due to a physiologic problem) is to place the food in front of the child and ignore the child regardless of what he or she does with the food. The parent might want to put a drop cloth underneath the chair of this child before presenting the food! Put the food down and carry on with the meal. Do not ask the child to eat and do not praise the child for eating. Eating should not become the focus or locus of a power struggle. This takes the naturalness out of eating. A child who is not eating strikes fear in the heart of the parent. Although picky eaters will eventually eat when they get hungry, resistant eaters may, in fact, not eat and become quite ill for lack of nutritional intake (Ernsperger & Stegen-Hanson, 2004).

Consistency in mealtimes is also important. As much as possible, parents should try to eat meals at the same time every day. This does not mean to the minute but rather, meals should be offered within the same hour each day. Extracurricular schedules do not always allow for consistent mealtimes, but if the daily schedule reflects the shift in time, and a snack is provided later in the day, dinner can be offered later to accommodate the soccer practice or band rehearsal. Preplanning is the key. Allowing children to participate in the planning of meals, preparation, and table setting may help with food issues.

Regardless of the reason a child becomes a resistant eater, there are treatment strategies available to help deal with this highly charged issue. However, parents are encouraged to realize from the moment of their child's diagnosis that eating can be a challenge and they are encouraged to deal assertively and effectively with this issue from the start (Ernsperger & Stegen-Hanson, 2004).

❖ Dietary Interventions? ❖

I wrote an article detailing some very positive behavioral changes in two young children with autism in 1997 (Adams & Conn, 1997). Way back then, all of 11 years ago, dietary interventions were being whispered about and many professionals, me included, treated our parents in a patronizing fashion, and noted the family to be "in denial." Those two children changed. They made eye contact. They began to speak spontaneously rather than just via echolalia. I watched them change. I documented their changes before, during, and after significant dietary changes had been implemented (gluten-free/casein-free [gf/cf]; megavitamins; nutritional supplements; yeast eradication treatment; Feingold diet). Granted, I was unable to determine which diet change did it or what combination of treatments turned things around, but what I was able to observe was both children "off diet" when they had consumed problem foods by accident. The rather rapid return of many "autistic" behaviors following consumption of a grain-filled cookie was evidence that could not be denied. I was never able to convince the parents or myself, for that matter, that a prolonged period of being off the diet would bolster our position that line of interventions helped. Suggesting that a mother feed her child the foods that may exacerbate the syndrome, and cause the child to stop talking or interacting, is tantamount to a sort of forbidden experiment. So the data would have been more compelling, but seeing it with my own eyes was convincing. I have seen many children improve on careful gf/cf diets.

That said, diet intervention is hard to do. It is expensive and not all foods are readily available. But, there are many more resources available to guide the family through shopping at the local grocery store. Lists of gf/cf safe foods are on the Internet. Books are available outlining how to alter the family diet with lots or recipes. Specialty foods and supplements are more readily available. Supplements are not controlled by the Food and Drug Administration. This makes them neither safe nor dangerous in and of themselves. However, many parents report meaningful changes in the quality of their child's life and their collective family life. Parents who implement a perfect diet, with no hidden gf/cf foods, should see improvements/changes in their child after about two weeks. Whether those changes will be of a magnitude that warrants continued devotion to such a precise treatment will be up to the family to determine. Parents report seeing continued growth and development up to 6 months into dietary interventions.

There are several theories that are associated diet intervention. The theory that related to the gf/cf diet is that persons with autism may have a metabolic disturbance that impacts their ability to successfully and safely metabolize wheat (gluten) and milk (casein) proteins. This incomplete metabolism allows gluten and casein to be turned into opioids or peptides that are found in the human and also in morphine, and then these substances impact the brain (Horvath, Papadimitiriou, Rabsztyn, Drachenberg, & Tildon, 1998; Reichelt, Knivsberg, Nodland, & Lind, 1994; Shattock, Kennedy, Rowell, & Berney, 1990). Although research is limited in this area, it is recognized as an important area for future study (Millward, Ferriter, Calver, & Connell-Jones, 2004). What must be understood is that the child cannot simply have less milk—he or she can have *no* milk. That means no milk protein in any form. A quick review of a can of vegetable soup will show whey as an ingredient. Whey is milk protein. Your child cannot simply have half a piece of wheat toast, he or she cannot have a molecule of wheat toast. It is this aspect of diet intervention that makes it most challenging, not impossible, but very challenging.

If you chose to attempt diet interventions, you have to be careful not to cross contaminate safe foods by preparing them or cooking them on the same surfaces, pots and pans where other nonsafe foods are handled. A parent with whom I work found that when she used the family fryer for her daughter's gf/cf foods, she had cross-contamination even though she used fresh oil. She surmised that perhaps the nonstick coating on the inside of the fryer might have harbored gluten. As a matter of her own peace of mind, the parent purchased cookware to be used specifically for her daughter's specialized diet.

Parents are also cautioned to keep as many nonsafe foods out of the house to begin with. I have worked with some older children who seem aware of their diet restrictions and actively avoid problem foods. For younger children, however, the distinction may not be meaningful so avoid temptation altogether by not having offending foods available. That said, you are now realizing how much is required of the family for dietary intervention to be effectively utilized.

❖ It's Potty Time ❖

Several factors can impact toilet training for children with ASD. These factors can include fear of the bathroom, and also the toilet itself. Some children have an extreme attraction to the toilet and will engage in repeated flushing. Often the transition from diapers to underwear causes upset and interferes with toilet training. Once the child begins to use the toilet, parents report that the child may urinate in the toilet but not use it for bowel movements and vice versa. Issues with toilet paper, hand washing, and other bathroom-related challenges can interfere with the development of independent toilet skills (Wheeler, 2004). Numerous resources are available to assist in the development of toilet skills. Ultimately, success will depend on the investment of time and patience on the part of the adults in the child's life. Consistency is the key to success in this as in most skills to be acquired by the child with ASD. When preparing for toilet training, the following factors must be considered. One must take into account communication needs, sensory awareness, need for routine, motor planning, anxiety, and response to new situations (Wheeler, 2004).

Some parents find placing a potty seat in the family living area to be effective in encouraging use. Some children do not want to be separated from the family and use the potty seat if it is in the common area. Perhaps the child has a fear of the flushing sound of the toilet and as a result, using the potty seat in another area may facilitate success. One aspect of toilet training that can give parents pause is the approach to the boy's need to stand. Traditional potty training has encouraged boys to sit on the potty to urinate. Later the child has to be retrained to stand for urination. Products are available that allow boys to stand from the start thereby eliminating the need for retraining. An Internet search should yield positive results for this type of equipment.

❖ The Space to Move ❖

Some families may have the luxury of space and be able to incorporate a sensorimotor room into the home. Even if a room cannot be given over to the equipment and materials needed for this type of activity, most families can find an area to dedicate. The types of materials and equipment may vary from child to child and be dependent on the sensory needs of the individual child. Many respond positively to rocking chairs, large therapy balls, and scooter boards. Many children also enjoy bouncing and swinging, but these can be placed outdoors in the form of a trampoline and swing set.

A big part of the sensory experience should be play. The job of the child is to play and one of the hardest things for children with ASD is to engage in what we call typical play. The child may pick up a ball, only to drop it on the ground and move on. A child with ASD with whom I worked years ago "taught" his father to throw a large ball up on the family carport so that it would roll off slowly in a fluid motion. Dad did this for hours on end and considered it play. Although his son enjoyed watching the ball, this could hardly be considered play in the truest sense of the word. However, with guidance and encouragement, the activity became interactive with the child learning to say "throw" and the father learning to help his child, with hand-over-hand assistance, and throw the ball to his sibling. Additionally, the ball became a basketball and was thrown into a hoop, making what had been a sensory stimulation activity into a play activity.

Families can engage an occupational therapist to assist in planning sensory activities, which should help the child develop play and communication skills, as well as motor development. Some caution is encouraged, however, when engaging in sensorimotor intervention. Although anecdotal information is abundant, research-based evidence is equivocal when it comes to whether children with ASD have sensory dysfunction (Rogers & Ozonoff, 2005). Sensory integration therapy (SIT) is a treatment approach developed in the 1970s that purports to address abnormal sensory functioning through vestibular, tactile, and proprioceptive stimulation. Many occupational therapists see SIT as a standard part of a comprehensive treatment program for ASD. It is important for parents to note that only four published studies exist that include objective data on SIT for children with ASD. Of the four, none demonstrated that SIT can impact the sensory concerns that might be related to ASD and none showed improvement in communication skill acquisition as is often mentioned when SIT is recommended (Case-Smith & Bryan, 1999; Linderman & Stewart, 1998; Ray, King, & Grandin, 1988; Reilly, Nelson, & Bundy, 1984). In a review of the available literature through the year 2000, Dawson and Watling noted that no conclusions about the effectiveness of SIT could be made given the paucity of research studies (Smith & Wick, 2008).

❖ Making Common Areas Work ❖

Children with ASD tend to be visual learners and, as a result, can be impacted by visual "clutter." Visual clutter is defined by the individual, but it if distracts and interferes with learning and functioning, it should be considered clutter. That said, it is essential that visual support strategies be used to facilitate learning and independence. So, how do you integrate visual supports and avoid visual clutter?

Parents should dedicate one area in the home, be that in the kitchen, dining area, living or family room, to the majority of visual support strategies. These should include daily schedules, calendars, and a list of the rules with consequences noted. Visual schedules and calendars are discussed more extensively in Chapter 4. Suffice it to say that, once crafted, those supports should be located in a common area that can be quickly referenced by all members of the family. An easy way to establish this control center is to either purchase or construct a combination cork and dry erase board. This combination should afford the maximum flexibility as it is recognized that things change with great rapidity in most families. The cork area can be used for the posting of a calendar, a daily schedule, and the rules. Let's talk about the importance of developing and posting of the rules.

Parents, grandparents, and other extended family members as well as other caregivers and even school personnel must collaborate to develop a list of rules that govern the behavior of all in the home. The rules should clearly and concisely define acceptable behavior. If cursing is not allowed, then a rule is posted to address this. If cleaning one's room every day is required, then post a rule to that effect. Posting the rules in all environments is essential. Many families find that merely verbally stating the rules is insufficient. Reliance on auditory memory and recall of rules is not usually conducive to successful following of the rules. Parents find themselves saying the same things over and over and over again. *Stop!* Develop a list of rules, write them down, and post them in the control center. In addition, copy the list onto cards and take them to other settings. All caregivers must have a list of the rules posted as well and must agree to adhere to the rules. Additionally, you may find that it is necessary to develop mini-rule lists for specific situations such as going to the park or the grocery store.

Consequences

A list of the consequences should be available in the command central area. This list is not restricted to punishments but also includes rewards to be doled out when desired behaviors are accomplished. It is essential that the same people who develop the rules also work together to develop consequences. Be sure to determine reasonable consequences for acceptable and unacceptable behavior. Adults tend to have less difficulty responding to inappropriate behavior, but we often forget to catch the children being good. If we want the child to repeat an appropriate behavior, we need to make sure we reinforce that behavior. Sometimes we spend so much time looking for and waiting for the problem behavior to occur, we forget to praise the acceptable behavior. A good target for all parents is to match each instance of negative consequence or punishment with two instances of positive reinforcement or praise. In other words, catch children being good twice as often as you catch them being bad.

❖ More Than a Bedroom ❖

Toys

The typical bedroom must provide the sleeping space for the child with the addition of toy storage. Toys can easily overwhelm the bedroom as most children have way too many toys.

It may seem rather harsh, but most children benefit from having no more than one basket or bin of toys. Having too many toys results in too little sustained attention and can seriously impact a child's ability to play.

For families who find they have already accumulated more than one basket of toys, a solution may be to rotate toys. After culling any broken or developmentally inappropriate toys from the collection, parents should obtain three or four baskets or bins. Similar items are placed in each basket so that each has cars, each has balls, each has dolls, and so on. After all the containers are filled, one is left in the room and the others are closed and stored. About every two to three weeks, the containers are switched. This allows toys to remain novel and stimulating for a longer period of time. This strategy also can facilitate cognitive development and flexibility of play.

Parents are also encouraged not to buy every toy on the market. It is natural to want to buy the newly diagnosed child many toys. Parents may feel the need to do this as a means of coping with what may be their own grief at receiving a challenging diagnosis. For that matter, parents just like to buy kids toys! At any rate, families are encouraged to keep it simple. Rather than buy many different cars and trucks, try to keep the number to less than 10. Rather than buy many different sets of farm animals, just buy one. Do not purchase every type of doll, just one baby doll and a couple of fashion dolls.

Decorating

Parents are encouraged to resist the temptation to decorate a bedroom with the child's favorite characters. It is understandable that a parent would want to fill the child's room with a favorite character as the child may not respond to many things. Parents want to feel that they are serving the child's needs by providing the child with things that are enjoyed. However, when one surrounds a child with one character in terms of décor and toys, one unwittingly perpetuates the child's limited interests. For example, if the child is interested in a certain animated train, it is *not* a good idea to buy all things related to the train. It is very difficult for a child to develop alternate interests when he or she is surrounded by only the train. When Jackson turned five, his parents said they wished they had not fed his obsession with farm animals by purchasing numerous animals sets and by decorating his room with farm animals. They said they realized that they had unwittingly nurtured his limited interests. A mom attending a workshop jokingly asked if she was wrong to have decorated her child's room with historical items and images since that was all he cared about now. Of course, she was most well intentioned, but in her zeal to make her child happy, she had played into his narrow interests. She also stated that she feared his interests would change soon as he had Asperger syndrome and his interest shifted frequently. She was worried that she would have to redecorate again very soon. She was encouraged to consider creating a very simple neutral background in her son's room to which she could add a few items related his current interest.

Labeling

To facilitate your child growth and development on the way to independence, label the drawers on the dresser with pictures and words. Label a drawer for socks, pajamas, t-shirts, and the like. The combination of words and pictures allows the child to recognize the picture icon first and then perhaps read the words later. Labeling shelves for the storage of books, movies, and containers is also helpful and with help your child can learn to mange his or her physical space. This is an important life skill that is often neglected as we tend to focus on things like communication and social skill development. Certainly, picking up ones toys does not rank as high in importance as communication, but it is a skill that will serve the child throughout his or her entire life.

❖ A Word About Siblings ❖

Parents are cautioned to make sure they devote special time and attention to the neurotypical siblings in the home. It is hard enough to be a brother or sister to begin with, but having a sibling with special needs can add more challenges. Many a sibling has reported feeling left out, rejected, put upon, and resentful toward their special needs sibling. These are all reasonable feelings for a child and to be expected. Parents must make sure they devote time to all their children. The neurotypical child is not being selfish when he or she wants to protect personal items and space. Some children with ASD can engage in destructive behaviors, so allow the non-ASD sibling to lock the bedroom. Parents must make sure they allot time and attention to the siblings. Every child needs special one on one time with Mom and Dad. It is all about the delicate balancing act of doling out time to the child with ASD and the non-ASD child.

Allow siblings to express their own anger and frustration without fear of retribution. It is hard to be the sibling of a special needs child. It is particularly hard to be the older brother or sister as often more responsibility for the special needs sibling falls to the older child. Parents should not expect or require caregiving by an older sibling. Should the older child offer, the parents can certainly accept, but this should be the choice of the older child. Younger siblings of special needs children may find that their developmental accomplishments go unacknowledged as the parents focus on seeing the same skill in the special needs child. Parents have shared with me stories of how their younger non-ASD child regressed back to a diaper after successfully being potty trained when the younger child noted that an older sibling with ASD was still in diapers.

❖ What IS on the TV? ❖

Don't assume your child can differentiate between TV and reality. A parent I met at a speaking engagement told about his son who believed a superhero to be a real person. The father explained that both the superhero and his alter ego were comic book characters, not real people. The child stated with great logic and exasperation,

"Dad, they have made three movies about him." This serves to illustrate the point better than anything I can say or a study can demonstrate. As a result, parents should be very cautious with regard to the content of television, movies, and the like to which they expose their children with ASD. Parents are encouraged to consider avoiding characters that gain control over others through physical confrontation. Expecting a child who has social deficits *not* to emulate a character who succeeds in obtaining what they want through force is not fair to the child. If the child cannot effectively separate fiction from reality, the child may chose to attempt to solve problems like their favorite superhero; that is, the child may chose to use force. This will be particularly problematic in daycare and school settings. It seems a small thing but it is vital that parents provide excellent role models for problem solving.

In addition to TV and such impacting problem-solving skills, these media also can serve to limit interests just as toys can. Children with ASD often become obsessed with certain cartoon characters, which then leads to the purchase of toys and decorating items related to that character. Some children's interest in cartoon characters will persist even when the characters are no longer developmentally appropriate for them. I work with a young teen who, at 13 years of age, was still playing with fashion dolls that were considered childish by her peers. She would attempt to discuss the dolls with her peers, but this led to her being more socially isolated. She recently shifted her interest to a popular movie musical and received positive feedback from her classmates.

❖ When Technology Does NOT Help ❖

Computers are useful tools for learning academic and communication skills (Herskowitz, 2008). In fact, computer-based vocabulary training was more effective than behavioral based treatment (Moore & Calvert, 2000). There is an emerging body of literature that indicates that computer-based instruction can be useful for the development of social interaction skills. Using animation to facilitate problem-solving, young children with autism were able to problem solve utilizing computer-based instruction (Bernard-Opitz, Sriram, & Nakhoda-Sapuan, 2001).

However, many children with ASD are extremely interested in computers and various programs or online activities that are not geared toward learning, communication or social skill development. Parents are cautioned to limit computer time and content. A child should be spending about 30 to 60 minutes on the computer each day. More than an hour a day on the computer means the child is not interacting with real people. Children with ASD need to interact with real people. If the child is using the computer to access information and activities related to a narrow interest, the computer has now become part of the obsession and its seemingly limitless content has been reduced. In this way, the computer has essentially been turned into a video game, a very expensive video game!

❖ What I Believe ❖

Movement and sensory activities are vital to the comprehensive programming for children with ASD. I wish the data were way more compelling, but they are not. I see the best outcomes in school-age children when their movement and sensory needs are addressed aggressively in the early grades, with consultative support as the child moves to middle and high school. Anecdotal information suggests that children with ASD benefit from the use of weighted blankets and vests. These are pricey items and not every family can afford to purchase them. With the help of my friend Lindsay, I was able to craft washable blankets for children at a preschool center who needed weighted blankets and vests. We collaborated to make blankets out of fabrics purchased at a local resale store. We made them out of ultrasuede and shiny satin-like polyester. We sewed two panels together (roughly 50" × 50") like a large pillow case leaving the top open initially. We then sewed channels from top to bottom about 6 inches wide. We then poured about ¼ to ⅓ cup of aquarium gravel into each channel. We then sewed across the blanket to form a 6 inch square. We added more gravel, sewed across again until we had made 6-inch squares all over the blanket. The result is a blanket that weighs between 3 and 5 pounds. The idea for aquarium gravel was novel and allows the blanket to be washed without necessitating the removal of the weights. Additionally, the gravel pieces are quite small and the children did not complain about how the gravel felt inside the blankets. We also made lap blankets and scarves that hang around the shoulders to facilitate sitting. Using a simple vest pattern, we made fashionable vests out of bright and happy fabrics. We included pockets on the inside of the vest to allow for the insertion of weights in plastic bags. The weights can be easily removed for washing. We used tie closures that could be tied into double bows to keep vests from being removed by the child.

I believe that, by the middle of middle school, the child with AS/HFA should be using keyboarding skills to access the curriculum. If the child has very poor handwriting by 5th grade, he or she will have the same in 6th grade and the academic demands of middle school will leave no time for improvement. The child needs to be able to sign his or her name. By the time he is an adult, he will likely never write a check . . . that will not be part of the future of these kids. They will be swiping cards left and right. Their technology future will be fundamentally different than perhaps any other generation. Many people with AS and HFA thrive in a technology-based class or workplace. I see this time as pivotal for a shift from pen/paper to a word processor, laptop, or other computer adaptation to the production of much of the academic coursework. This removes a potential meltdown situation for many on the spectrum. Handwriting is such a laborious task for so many. The coordination of listening, reading, thinking, answering, and writing is potentially cognitively overwhelming. What can be removed from this "meltdown" recipe is the handwritten work.

I believe we live with much chaos in our lives. No, not from the child with ASD, but chaos from the clutter and stuff we surround ourselves with. I believe less is more. I am one of those hyperorganized types and I know where everything is and I have little, if any, excess stuff. I am a donator. Go through your house and clear out all the physical clutter. This means every closet, every cabinet, every nook and cranny. Do not try this all in one day. Take one room at a time. Be ruthless in that your emotional attachment to things should not get in the way of clearing out clutter. If your child has tons of stuffed animals that all have a memory for you, take a photo of the fuzzy friend, label it with the giver, event, and so on, and then pass it on if it is in good shape. If it is not, then discard it in as ecofriendly a way as possible. Contact your local municipality to determine how to recycle old electronics and computers. Find out where a clothing closet is and take your gently used clothes so others can benefit from them. There are now more consignment stores open for children's clothes, furniture, and toys so you can sell your items if you want.

Streamline. Simplify. Your world will be very full as you try and raise your child with ASD, and you need to have a clear, breathable space to do that. Find a place for everything and label that space with a picture and/or print so you know where things go. This also allows children to be more active participants in putting things away.

I believe that some kids on the spectrum probably should not be watching a great deal of fantasy, superhero type stuff. Some kids cannot make the distinction between reality and pretending. A child who has problems moving through the social world probably should not focus on characters who overcome by force/power/great strength. This problem-solving strategy does not work at school, in the park, or at work. These kids need us to help them learn to comport themselves. We have to model what we want them to demonstrate. I have been a TV watcher since childhood, so I get the appeal. Just make careful, informed choices about what your child watches. Finally, I suggest not facilitating a child's desire to watch one video repeatedly. I am not sure much good comes of it although it often does increase delayed and mitigated echolalia, which can be shaped into more conventional language.

I believe computers and video games have their place in entertaining and educating kids on the spectrum. I think computer use must be monitored. I think educational games and Internet sites are wonderful resources for successfully raising a child with ASD. But I believe they may be a parent's most powerful reinforcer, so Mom, Dad, you have to be in control of what Dr. Phil calls the "currency." Use the computer as a reward for good work at school or good behavior at the store. Remember that the computer and video games are often solitary activities and, although your children may truly enjoy playing games by themselves, they should not be allowed to do so for extended periods of time. Thirty to 60 minutes of gaming daily is more than enough for most children on the autism spectrum.

I believe there is a lot of wisdom in watching the nanny reality shows. Those nannies make sure the house is orderly, that kids have chores or responsibilities, and the nannies always *post the rules*. They all stress the importance of consistency in terms of expectations and consequences. Any time you need a dose of Parenting 101, watch a nanny show.

Many of us grew up eating a great deal of processed foods. I recently discovered organic foods. They are better for me, I believe. You may not be able to go completely gf/cf but following the Feingold diet or something similar could be a good alternative. Less chemical exposure seems to be good for kids with ASD—or at least not bad for them. I think it is worth a try!

CHAPTER 4

Seeing Is Believing

❖ Visual Schedules ❖

From the time the child is diagnosed with ASD until the day he leaves the planet, he needs a schedule. That may sound dramatic, and it is. We all use schedules and most of us cannot make it through the day without referencing our to-do list. That is what a schedule is, our to-do list. Schedules allow us to move from one event to the next. They allow us to transition easily. They allow us to know what is coming next. For the child with ASD, this aspect of schedule use may be the most critical. Knowing what is coming next is often anxiety-inducing in the child with ASD. The child may love music time in the preschool center but may worry and be anxious that music will not occur. Being able to reference the schedule lets the child know that music will come. The child may be able to relax and enjoy the current activity knowing that music time is just ahead. The materials needed to make a schedule include poster board, hook and loop tape, objects, photos or pictures, an envelope or cup for completed events, and perhaps lamination film.

Object Schedules

When the child is younger than age three, you may need to start with objects on the schedule. This may require placing a spoon on a card to represent mealtime. A block hot-glued to a card can be the symbol for playtime. Once the schedule is created, it must be used every day. This is essential to the development of this life skill. If the use of the schedule is inconsistent, so the effectiveness of the schedule also will be inconsistent. The schedule should be referenced immediately before an event is to occur. Once the event is concluded, the symbol is removed from the schedule. This demonstrates for the child that the event is completed and it is time to move to the next event.

Once the child has gained some facility with the object schedule, one can pair photos of the events with the objects to gradually fade the objects from the schedule. Print should always be paired with items on the schedule. The child is not expected to read, but pairing pictures and print will help with the transition to a print-based schedule later.

Now that the schedule has been created and is being used consistently, use it to address such things as transition problems. If the child does not want to stop center play, the child is taken to the schedule, the picture of center time is removed, and the child is directed to the next item. Sometimes, it is helpful to have the child carry the symbol of the event to that event. For example, the child may carry the symbol for lunch to the lunch room. Upon finishing lunch, the picture is returned to the envelope, cup, or box where completed events are stored. It is vital that the schedule be ready for the child's use at the start of each day. Some find it helpful to place the first item on the schedule and then enlist the help of the child in the ordering and placement of the remaining events.

Minischedules

In addition to all-day schedules, minischedules can be very useful for the successful completion of tasks. Minischedules are created in the same fashion as all-day schedules. A minischedule serves to illustrate all the steps in a particular task. Take tooth brushing for example. This seemingly simple task includes several steps that must be completed in order for success. The minischedule delineates all the steps so that toothpaste is placed on the toothbrush prior to brushing. This is not meant to be condescending. Parents tell me all the time that their incredibly bright child cannot recall all the steps in simple tasks. Minischedules facilitate independence. Some adults with Asperger syndrome report using minischedules in their everyday lives for things like laundry and personal hygiene.

To Photograph or Not to Photograph

The question of using photos versus line drawings often arises. Some children can transition from objects to colored line drawings without great difficulty. Others may need to use actual photos after objects before eventually moving to line drawings. Parents can purchase computer software that provides either photos or line drawings. Several resources are available for the creation of visual schedules. Software packages are available that create both photos and line drawings. A frequent question regarding using photos relates to whether the photo should depict the child in the actual event. Parents are cautioned about using photos of their children in actual scenes as this may create a limiting symbol. The child may only acknowledge the photo as meaningful when the situation is identical to the photo. For example, a parent created a minischedule for shoe tying for her son with ASD. He used it successfully but only to tie the shoes depicted in the photos. He did not generalize the skill to other shoes. This may seem an unlikely outcome but others report similar difficulties when they used specific photos.

Portable, Accessible, and Functional

Sometimes, the visual schedule needs to be portable. A small dry erase or cork board can serve as a portable schedule. Events can be listed on the dry erase board and crossed off or erased as events are completed. Printed pictures could be taped to the board. One could affix the loop portion of the tape to the board and place small pictures there. It matters less how one goes about creating the portable board than the fact that one is created and utilized.

Another concern is accessibility. The schedule must be readily accessible for the child to reference, but sometimes, the child will manipulate the schedule to avoid an undesired event. When the child is young, it is important for the adult to remove the symbols/pictures after each event. Once the child becomes a little older or demonstrates that he or she will adhere to the established order, he or she can then be allowed to remove the pictures. Some persons with ASD will not be able to manage their schedules independently but this should be a goal, even if it is a long-term goal.

A variation of the visual schedule strategy is the use of picture lists for trips to the grocery store or local department store. To keep the child focused on the task at hand and to encourage participated, parents can create a shopping list for the child. If the child can read, print is used. If not, the use of pictures or even product labels glued to an index card can suffice. The child now has a job to do. That is to find all the items on her shopping list. The list can also be helpful in diverting attention from items that the parent does not want to purchase. It may be helpful to say "We have to buy what is on our lists. We can't buy things that are not on the list. That is the rule." Parents who have used this technique report that it can be effective.

❖ Structure But Not Rigid Routine ❖

A caveat to the use of visual schedules is this. Schedules basically are an ordered list of how we hope things should go. This does not mean that things won't change at the last minute. The beauty of an interchangeable schedule format is that the change can be made relatively easily. Furthermore, it is important to iterate and reiterate that what one is seeking is structure from the schedule but not adherence to a rigid routine. No one is well served by doing everything everyday at the same time and in the same order. Structure is the goal. There should be a schedule that shows what the structure of the day will be but varying tasks and their order should be considered. Many parents report that their child wants everything to be the same every day. This is part of ASD and is to be expected. No one with ASD benefits from having every day be the same. Certainly, it is understandable that a predictable order of events can reduce anxiety. However, leading a child to believe that every day will be the same is not fair to the child. Living successfully in the real world requires all of us to encounter and deal with the unexpected. Making everything the same is easier than making everything realistic, but realism is required.

Mix things up as much as possible. Have a schedule for each day but not the same schedule every day. Reference the schedule often. Direct your child to check his schedule frequently. The idea is that the child will learn to look at the schedule on his own and will learn to use the schedule as a tool for keeping focused and for reducing anxiety. Schedules are a lifelong support strategy. Do not stop using a schedule, just adapt to whatever type of schedule is needed as the child grows and matures. As a psychiatrist specializing in autism told me recently "Taking the schedule away from a child is tantamount to kicking the crutch out from under the child with a broken leg."

Having a child on the autism spectrum requires structure. Bedtime routines are important. Bedtime should be consistent but not cut in stone as sometimes things happen. I worked with a boy whose parents recalled travel home one evening from an event and the child noted that it was bedtime according to the clock in the car. He became extremely upset as his nightly ritual was being disrupted. No amount of reassurance would calm him and the last

15 minutes of the drive home was miserable. Ultimately, routine and ritual walk a fine line. Build in flexibility. Be careful assigning specific times to schedules. It is more important to note the order of events rather that the time of the events. Many a child has gotten unwanted attention in school because he or she pointed out that the teacher's schedule said spelling ended at 9:35. As it was now 9:37, spelling must be over and no more spelling can occur. This does not endear the child to the teacher. So a word to teachers, avoid times on your schedules!

❖ Social Stories ❖

The use of social stories as a supplemental treatment strategy is gaining a fair amount of empirical support in the professional literature (Adams, Gouvousis, VanLue, & Waldron, 2004; Simpson, 2005). Social stories are a noninvasive approach that can provide the social script children with ASD need to navigate a variety of situations. The stories provide the child with information about the situation, what it looks like, how they should behave, and how they will know that they are on track. Social stories consist of descriptive sentences (The teacher says when it is time for lunch. The children stop working when it is time for lunch.); directive sentences (I am working at my desk. The teacher says that it is time for lunch. I stop working when it is time lunch.); perspective sentences (The teacher smiles when all the children stop working and get ready for lunch.); and control sentences (I stop working and get ready for lunch when the teacher says to. When the teacher says to stop working, it is time for lunch.).

Social stories can be written to address situations as broad as going to a store to those as specific as walking in line from the classroom to the lunchroom. Social stories can be written by anyone willing to take the time to observe the situation, observe the child in the situation, observe others in the situation, observe when confusion on the part of the child may occur, and so forth. There are now a number of generic social stories published in books that can be easily adapted to meet the individual needs of children with ASD. Parents are cautioned not to pull a prepared story out of a book, read it to the child, and expect it to "work." Generic stories are nonspecific, hence generic, and may not meet the unique needs of the child in the specific situation encountered. Take the story and adjust it to meet the needs of your child in your life circumstance.

❖ Other Visual Supports ❖

Checklists

Certainly, we have all made a list of things that we have to do. Perhaps our lists name chores or tasks that we hope to accomplish over a week's time. For the child with autism or Asperger syndrome, the list might be for things that the child needs to accomplish in the next hour. If the child is in study hall, the checklist may include the list of assignments facing the child. The child may complete the items and check them off the list. Later, the list may be referenced again at home to ensure that all assignments are completed prior to the next school day.

For maximum flexibility, dry erase boards are available in all shapes and sizes. Many boards come with magnets allowing them to be placed on home appliances or inside a school locker. Items can be checked or marked off the list and the boards can be easily erased and a new list created as needed. The markers for such boards also come in a variety of colors allowing color coding of tasks to facilitate organization. School-related tasks might be written in red, while play or sports related tasks could be written in blue. This makes the list easily scanned by adults and help children learn to categorize similar tasks or events.

To facilitate participation in daily living activities, checklists allow the child to help with shopping or other errands. For example, the child can be given a pen and the grocery list for which she is responsible. She checks off the items as they are purchased, making her essential to successful shopping. This can also occupy the child's attention, reducing distractions that might cause aberrant behavior. When the family has a number of errands to run, it is important that the child be kept involved and busy. Giving the child a card with the names of all the stores to be visited allows her to remain focused and helps her know when the errands will be completed (Adams, 2007).

Cue Cards

When the child with ASD is faced with delivering a verbal message, the stress of the situation may impact the child's ability to transmit that message. A cue card allows the child to relay a message by referencing the card. The child can use the card as a cue to assist in transmitting the verbal message, or if that proves too challenging the child can simply pass the card to their communication partner (Janzen, 2003). Cue cards can be printed for a variety of situations, color coded for topics, laminated, a hole punched, and then placed on a "c" ring. The ring allows for the easy addition or removal of cards. It also allows the cards to be clipped to the child's belt loop or book bag. Cue cards can be expanded to include a short list of options for addressing a social situation, like how to enter a conversation. The key to using the cue card is not to overwhelm the user with excessive information or language. Keep it clear and concise. A situation that might lend itself to cue cards is greeting a new person. The cue card contains the language needed for the greeting and helps the child know that he has been successful in the exchange. It also lets him know when the exchange is completed (Adams, 2007). I work with a number of older teens and adults who have cue cards for things like greetings and eye contact. Although these skills have been targeted for years in some cases, they have never become automatic. Cue cards serve to help the person remember all those things they have to do to be a social person.

Color-Coded Materials

To address executive function issues, color-coded materials may prove helpful. Families and teachers are encouraged to utilize systems using color to help the child with autism develop and maintain self-management skills. Using colored file folders and closable colored plastic sleeves, the child's schoolwork can be organized by subject. Placing the file folder for assignment pages, worksheets, homework, a notebook, and pencils/pens in the plastic sleeve, along with texts and workbooks creates a manageable packet the child can retrieve for each class or subject.

This is particularly helpful when children with autism enter the later elementary grades, middle and high school where they have to change classes and have more materials to keep up with. By placing a legend on the child's desk or inside the locker, the child can match the appropriate packet for the next class. At the end of the day, the child can place the packets needed for homework or other classwork in the book bag to take home.

For the home, color coding on a monthly calendar can help the child with autism know which days are school days and which are not. Using colored adhesive disks, the parents and child can place one color on school days and another color on weekends and holidays. This can be particularly helpful as teacher workdays can disrupt a child's rhythm. Most schools announce workdays and holidays well in advance allowing for this type of planning. Additional colors can be added for sports, therapies, and other daily or weekly events. Color coding allows children with autism and Asperger syndrome to develop self-management skills, learning to prepare themselves for the days events by recognizing the colors (Adams, 2007).

❖ What I Believe ❖

I believe that visual schedules are one of the most important visual support strategies a parent can use. I believe they are an essential part of any intervention program. A person with ASD can and will learn to manage his or her life with the use of a schedule. Parents should not make the common mistake that many professionals have made, that is, removing the schedule when the child seems to have the schedule memorized. This frequently happens in schools. Teachers report that the child has the class schedule committed to memory and the schedule is abandoned. This may seem a reasonable thing but don't unexpected events occur at school? Don't we have special events or cancellations that are not expected? It is on these days that the schedule is needed and if it has been put away or worse yet, discarded, it is not readily available for use in managing the disruption.

Here is an exercise for parents. Imagine for a moment that you have lost your planner or datebook or that your electronic calendar has crashed. *Really* think about this for a bit. How do you feel? Are you getting anxious? Are you becoming concerned that you will miss an appointment? Are you beginning to panic? Perhaps this is how your child feels when he or she cannot predict what will happen next.

Use visual supports liberally. Use whatever you need to use to make your child's life and by association, your life easier. Color code things. Label everything. Put pictures on everything. Make sure you pair print and pictures so you can make the transition to print only whenever it is appropriate for your child's developmental level. Make lists with pictures for the store. If somebody looks at you funny because of all the visual supports, let them.

I believe social stories are one of the best tools for providing a person with ASD the script they need for nearly any social situation. Social stories can be written to address issues as basic as how to put on shoes and socks to those as complex as how to behave at a concert at the local symphony. Social stories do not change a child's brain chemistry, do not require a master's degree to write, and they work. Write them, use them, and read them often. Share them with others who interact with the child. Do not wait for your child to have a problem in a new situation. Anticipate the possibility and write a story before the situation occurs.

CHAPTER 5

School Days, School Days!

❖ Proactive Planning ❖

I got an e-mail from a young mother whose son with autism began PreK two days ago. Well, day one was terrific. On day two, however, he hit the teacher, was yelling and shaking his fists at his friends. She asked what she should do and I thought "Why didn't she know what to do before school started?" and then I thought "Why didn't the school help prepare the child and his family for this major life change?" I realized no one is at fault; they are all just stuck in the "reactive" mode. Information is power. Information allows you to be ready. Information allows you to be proactive.

Be Prepared

This young child should have had a number of social stories available to address the many challenges of PreK including rules, play, sharing, and the like. He is a verbal child but it is well known that in moments of high stress, the child may have difficulty accessing his verbal skills. He may resort to a more primitive response (hitting). This should not be unexpected in this situation. It should have been anticipated by all, and all must realize that this too shall pass. Given the appropriate supports and assistance, this child probably will adapt to his new school world relatively quickly.

In addition to the social stories, which provide the scripts for school, this child initially will need support from the teacher and perhaps the local speech-language pathologist (SLP) in order to access his existing language and to develop the language of school. Even verbal children with HFA can demonstrate communication challenges in the classroom at the start of a new school year. Expect transition issues in children with ASD at the start of every school year, and especially when the school itself changes.

Middle School Preparation

The change from elementary to middle school can be the most challenging for those with HFA and AS. The social world of middle school is stressful, maddening, and confusing to those not on the spectrum. Add ASD to the mix and recognize that this is a time when children on the spectrum may be most vulnerable. While trying to navigate this social environment, children with AS/HFA often find themselves experiencing academic challenges. Many of these children found minimal challenge in the academic aspect of elementary school. Couple the social quagmire with frustration in math and the result can be explosive. Adding hormonal fuel to this fire just ratchets everything up a notch.

Now that the image of a 6th-grade boy with AS is blazing in your brain, what should happen before he enters middle school? Hopefully, he has a personal calendar/planner or even a personal digital assistant (PDA) that houses his schedule, and family contact information. He should have made at least one dry run through the school moving from room to room as noted on his class schedule. He should have met all his teachers. He should know where he is going to sit before the first day. He should have the school rules written out and taped to this notebook. He should have his personal cue cards (e.g., Raise my hand. Ask for help) written out and easily accessible. He should know where the counselor's office is located and maybe even the school nurse. He needs to know where he can go if he finds himself feeling overwhelmed and in need of some down time. He should have an IEP or 504 plan in place that details his academic, social, and behavioral accommodations and interventions and *all* should be in place and working from the first bell of the day.

High School Challenges

High school is even more of a challenge to those with AS and HFA. Social issues will remain but will have morphed into new issues. Academic challenges will likely continue, the same but different. I cannot tell you that high school won't be a challenge, but I can tell you that if you have been consistent in your expectations of your child's behavior and if you have provided structure and support along the way, you will make it through to graduation. Although I know of no specific data to support this premise, I do believe that children with AS/HFA who have had early intervention, consistent parenting, communication support, and structure will have greater success in college.

So the bottom line here is that you have to plan ahead. Parents must work with the school personnel to make sure that supports are in place to support success. You have to share information ahead of time. You have to be ready to change plans when it becomes apparent (and it will) that you guessed wrong on a couple of things, but you still will have gotten most of things right. You have to be patient as the child finds a way to assimilate, accommodate, and finally adapt. If you put a sound foundation in place, the child will be able to build on it.

❖ Advocating for Your Child ❖

Contrary to what many may report, this is not a case of you against the school. The family and school must collaborate. Everyone must be on the same page with regard to the needs of the child. Parents cannot ask the school to use a strategy or behavior management technique that is not in keeping with school policy. For example, some parents utilize corporal punishment. Many schools no longer allow this type of intervention for behavioral concerns. It is vital that the behavior management system used at school and at home be consistent. Inconsistency results in disruptive behavior. Two sets of expectations result in disruptive behaviors. If I child is allowed to turn lights on and off repetitively at home, he is likely to try and engage in the same behavior at school. He will not be able to do this at school. Frankly, he does not need to be doing it at home either. It is a nonfunctional activity that has no correlate in the real world. As far as I know, there are no jobs that require switching lights on and off. Turning lights off and on at school generally is not appreciated by the classroom teacher. Extinguishing this behavior at home will benefit the child at school and in other contexts.

Once the school and family have collaborated on a behavior plan, that plan must be integrated into the academic plan for the child. One must understand that academic demands trigger behavior concerns. It is inappropriate to have separate academic and behavior plans. If this is offered, it is indicative of a lack of understanding of the interaction of academics and behavior. I have encountered instances where the teacher has focused on a problem behavior but has not recognized that a classroom demand triggered the problem behavior. I have encountered parents who have failed to recognize that their child can have few behavior challenges at home while having many at school.

Parents need to understand that school can trigger problem behaviors and should not be surprised when they get troubling reports from school. What parents cannot assume is that the school is not trying to meet the needs of their child. The school should not assume that the parents are in denial if they state that these problems do not occur at home. After the initial period right after diagnosis, school is probably the hardest time for parents of children with ASD.

Patience is a Virtue

Now, the reality check is that many in schools are well intentioned but not trained to deal with children with ASD. Although ASD is now diagnosed in 1 out of every 125 children, training of school personnel has not necessarily kept pace with this surge. Additionally, children with HFA and AS are among the most challenging students to educate. Classroom teachers often are not prepared for the student who can recite science facts, but not tolerate minor changes in the daily class schedule. Many teachers are confused when a kindergarten child can read, but does not follow simple directions. Children with HFA/AS generally are enrolled in regular education classes, often with little need for special education support beyond resource class assistance. This happens because the latest emulation of the public law, Individuals with Disabilities Education Act (IDEA), and the policy of No Child Left Behind (NCLB) states that a diagnosis of autism does not automatically result in the development of an individualized education plan (IEP). Unless a child's autism results in academic difficulties, the child may not qualify for an IEP.

Tiers not Tears

Although policies vary from state to state, most schools are implementing response to intervention (RTI) or "tiers" for providing intervention and support to determine whether or not an IEP needs to be developed. The integral part of this approach is what is referred to as the tiers. Tier one takes place in the regular classroom setting and is what teachers do every day, which is to differentiate their teaching to try and meet the learning needs of all in the class. Tier one requires that teachers try a variety of strategies, documenting the strategy and the response in lesson plans. If the student continues to have difficulties, Tier two interventions are implemented. At this tier, the student may participate in smaller group activities with an interventionist. For example, local schools in southern Georgia have a team of interventionists who implement small group activities for those identified as being as risk for language and learning difficulties. Should this level of intervention not prove to be of sufficient benefit, the student is then moved to Tier three. It is at Tier three that screenings may take place along with more specialized interventions, which often are implemented by the school specialists, the speech-language pathologist or occupational therapist. If warranted, a child may be referred to Tier four, where a full-scale assessment is completed and an IEP developed.

Several states have implemented rulings that state that children with a formal diagnosis of ASD do not have to go through the RTI process. That should not be interpreted to mean that a child with ASD will automatically receive an IEP and special education services. What this means is that the child can move directly to the assessment process to determine if the child qualifies for special education services. Recall that the child's deficits have to have an educational impact in order for an IEP to be developed. This point is particularly important relative to students with HFA/AS. This student may not present with test scores and performance measurements that allow him or her to be found eligible for special education services. Careful assessment by the right professionals, with the right tools in the right contexts is essential to ensure that the student with HFA/AS is truly not eligible for services. An essential part of the assessment process is test administration. Tests generally are administered in a quiet setting, one on one. This is not the learning environment where the student must function; therefore, it is essential that some level of assessment occur in the classroom setting.

The "Hidden Curriculum"

Another aspect of the school and community at large that impacts the child with ASD is what is referred to as the "hidden curriculum" (Myles & Simpson, 2003). The hidden curriculum refers to the slang of the students, and the rules that "everyone knows" but that are not explicitly stated. One teacher allows quiet discussion in the room whereas another does not, but neither teacher has those rules posted. The child with ASD is not likely to understand what behaviors are pleasing to the teacher, as the child with ASD is egocentric in his thinking, and does not know the teacher needs to be pleased. The hidden curriculum of the community includes things like not talking to strangers, but a policeman is a stranger and if he is asking the child with ASD a question, he is expecting an answer. Children with ASD usually have all or nothing rules, very black and white distinctions that do not allow for exceptions (Myles & Simpson, 2001).

❖ Interventions for School ❖

Only a few intervention strategies have been evaluated for effectiveness in the classroom setting. The only model developed specifically for the classroom is the TEACCH (Treatment and Education of Autistic and Communication-handicapped Children) approach. The TEACCH model for intervention was developed in North Carolina and is used with great success around the world. Randall and Parker (1999) chose the TEACCH model as a desirable model over others because of the following characteristics: respect for the person with autism, respect for the parents and families of the person with autism, inclusion of the caregivers in all aspects of treatment planning and service delivery, in-depth knowledge of autism as it impacts all aspects of child development by professional personnel, open mindedness of personnel, long term data to support the approach, a comprehensive program serving the person with autism into adulthood, and adaptability of the approach as evidenced by its adoption in non-English speaking countries. In a nutshell, the TEACCH approach emphasizes teaching children to communicate many meanings, with many purposes in a variety of contexts. It is representative of a melding of behavioral and psycholinguistic approaches (Watson, Lord, Schaffer, & Schopler, 1989).

TEACCH is not a technique or even a collection of techniques. It is a model for comprehensive treatment delivery that allows for the development of treatment plans based on an individual's specific needs, as opposed to a one-size-fits-all checklist. TEACCH lists as its main objective the improvement in communication skills and autonomy so that the person with autism can reach his or her maximum potential. Rather than focusing on behaviors, as most behavior modification programs do, the TEACCH model serves to address the underlying causes of the aberrant behaviors, thereby increasing adaptation and lessening behavior difficulties. The result of this approach is that the person with autism can begin to better communicate wants and needs and recognize that he or she can impact the behavior of others effectively to get needs met. Additionally, by beginning with a simple atmosphere of success, we can gradually increase the complexity of the tasks and the environment, we can increase autonomy.

TEACCH relies heavily on the notion of visual supports as the visual modality can be preferred by children with ASD. TEACCH programming includes structure that does not allow for down time in the classroom. The model stresses the importance of the child being engaged in activities, not sitting passively. Each child has a workstation that includes an "In" box and "out" box or "Finished" box. The student completes the required work, moves it to the out or finished box. When the in box is emptied a play break is earned. TEACCH also includes prompts such as "First . . . then" meaning first you work, and then you play. The model includes workboxes that can house fun activities or learning activities, but a number are available so that the student is constantly engaged in learning. Although the TEACCH model may not move as rapidly as some discrete trial training (DTT) programs, there is some support for the notion that when a child initiates learning on his own, without as much prompting and cueing as can occur in DTT programming, the child becomes a more independent learner (Siegel, 2008).

Contrary to popular belief, DTT, Lovaas approach, and the like have not been extensively tested in the school setting. DTT has been shown to improve outcomes when it is implemented in a home-based, intensive (approximately 40 hours per week) program, started prior to age 5 years, and lasting for at least 2 years. What some have done is taken the success of DTT and attempted to translate it into a school setting. Although DTT should be expected to help with some skill acquisition, the idea that its use in schools has been evaluated is not born out by the existing literature. That said, one should recognize that DTT is limited in its empirical support beyond age 5 and caution should be used when attempting to use it in a classroom setting.

❖ IFSP and IEP Is Not Alphabet Soup! ❖

IDEA, the federal law governing the education of children with specials needs, mandates two documents depending on the age of the child. For children younger than 36 months of age, the Individualized Family Service Plan (IFSP) is the legally required document. The IFSP is developed to address the family's needs, not just those of the child. The parents are actively involved in the crafting of the IFSP, particularly with regard to the description of the family's strengths and needs, as well as the objectives to be met for the family and the child with special needs. The sections of the IFSP include: a detailed history, the current status of the family and child, family resources, priorities and concerns, the desired outcomes, and the services to be provided. If the child is nearing the third birthday, the plan requires a plan to be in place to facilitate the transition to the school for continued services. Although IDEA mandates the IFSP, schools may not be the agency providing the services. Services for the birth to three population often are provided by early intervention agencies, private practitioners, and the like.

Elementary School and Beyond

For the school-age child (3–21 years), the required document is the Individualized Education Program or IEP. The IEP requires the participation of the parents in the development of annual goals and objectives. The IEP must include a description of the child's present level of performance in academics and other areas including communication, motor skill development, and so forth. It must also contain measurable goals and objectives that are designed to meet the student's needs as they arise from the disability, and how progress will be measured. The IEP also states what services the student will receive, how frequently, and from whom. Additional sections include the extent to which a child will participate in the regular education curriculum and any accommodations deemed necessary for local- and state-level assessments. Often, alternate assessment procedures are used including portfolio assessments. These take the place of the standardized tests that may be required by the state or district to determine skill mastery and promotion.

Some children do not qualify for and IEP because, although they have a medical diagnosis of autism or Asperger syndrome, the severity of the disorder is such that it does not cause academic challenges. In this instance, the student may qualify for a 504 plan under the Americans with Disabilities Act of 1990. This is often referred to as the "other health impaired" category. I have found that many with HFA and AS do not qualify for IEPs but do need specific accommodations and therefore need a 504 plan. It is important to note that, although every student with an IEP has a right to a 504 plan, students who have 504 plans do not automatically qualify for an IEP.

❖ Extended School Year and ❖ Regression/Recoupment

Not every child with ASD will qualify for an extended school year (ESY). ESY allows for summer programming for a child with special needs. This is not the same a summer school, which is a program for remediation to support promotion. ESY is determined to be appropriate when a child is on the verge of accomplishing learning or new skill acquisition at the end of the school year and the lack of continued schooling would cause this opportunity to be lost. Another justification for ESY is if the child demonstrated significant regression after the summer break and the recoupment or recovery of those lost skills took longer than the expected first four to six weeks back. Most children show some time to recover skills that were not practiced over the summer. If the recoupment period is much greater than expected or if skills are not recovered, ESY should be considered.

What is most important in this situation for parents to understand is that summer is not the time to stop all the things that worked during the school year. Schedules need to be in place. Plenty of hands-on, functional, meaningful activities should be part of the daily experience of the child so as to maintain skills. Teachers will tell you that they observe regression just over a week break if the home situation does not provide ample support, structure, and opportunity for practice of skills.

❖ **What I Believe** ❖

I believe that, for the most part, the public schools are well intentioned in their attempts to provide meaningful learning experiences
for children with ASD. I believe that "well intentioned" may not
translate into the implementation of effective assessment or treatment strategies. Public schools in the United States have huge
responsibilities in the educational of all students and are woefully
underfunded, understaffed, and undersupported. IDEA is not fully
funded. It never has been yet it is the federal law governing the
land of special education. NCLB is the biggest unfunded mandate
to come along in years. Although the idea of NCLB is a nice one
that makes us feel good about education, the policy is forcing
schools to teach to tests, and suck most of the joy out of teaching.
If a regular education teacher has a student with ASD in her classroom and that student impacts the learning of others, the teacher
may resent that student's presence in the classroom. Remember, the
teacher's continued employment may be predicated on her students'
test scores at the end of the school year. Anything that can impact
those scores is problematic. Add to that the fact that the teacher
probably received little or no training on how to teach students
with ASD, and you have a recipe for potential problems.

I believe that schools may be vulnerable to purchasing prepack-
aged, one-size-fits-all intervention programs that have little empirical support. These programs are attractive because they are often
computer-based, allowing the child to work alone on the computer,
requiring minimal adult intervention and supervision, thereby cost-
ing less money overall.

I believe parents have to take responsibility for and be fully
invested in following up on techniques and strategies that work at
school. If they work at school, use them at home. If you expect the
school system to be able to teach your child any sustainable skills
without reinforcing the skills at home, you are fooling yourself and
short changing your child. If you expect to drop your child off at
school each day and if you expect all that is learned at school to
immediately generalize to the home, you will be disappointed. The
reverse is true as well. If you expect skills demonstrated at home to
instantly transfer to school, you are in for a letdown.

I believe the *only* way a child with ASD will be a successful learner and participant is if the parents and school and other professionals work together with open honest communication and reasonable expectations. That means parents must make sure they participate in every decision that impacts their child. That means that parents must educate themselves with regard to what treatments can be expected to work for their child. That means that the schools must be willing to provide trained and qualified staff to provide empirically sound treatment. I feel certain that the school wants to provide quality services but is hampered by lack of funding and salaries that have not kept pace with the innumerable demands of the classroom.

CHAPTER 6

Talking, Playing, Doing, Being!

❖ Communication Development ❖

Communication development begins at birth and continues until death. Although that seems a dramatic statement, it serves to illustrate the premise that this life skill must be addressed throughout the life of the child with ASD and not just during the early years. A brief review of early speech and language development is included here to provide the reader with a reference for typical development. Without a reference point, it is a challenge to recognize what "normal" might be and without a "normal model" to follow, one cannot frame an effective treatment plan.

I Am Born

At birth, the neurotypical infant is "prewired" for speech and language acquisition. The baby responds best to the human voice. His hearing is tuned for the pitches and frequencies associated with human speech. Babies, as young as 20 minutes of age, demonstrate something called entrainment. Entrainment is the rhythmic head nodding that is elicited from the neonate only in response to human speech. It cannot be elicited through rhythmic tapping or environmental sounds (Owens, 2005). The typical neonate focuses on the eyes of the caregiver rather than a random facial feature. This is of particular interest given the recent findings that seem to indicate that children who were later diagnosed with ASD were less likely to look at other people and seek them out, and were less likely to smile and vocalize to others in the first 6 months (Maestro et al., 2001).

By 6 to 11 months of age, the neurotypical infant is able to engage in what is referred to as canonical or reduplicated babbling. An example of this type of babbling is the repetition of a syllable (mamamamama). Until this time, the child made sounds that *felt* good. The child engages in canonical babbling because it *sounds* good. Therefore, this stage of babbling may be considered more important as it may indicate a shift to a higher cognitive function. At about 8 months of age, the child may engage in "echolalic speech" or "echolalia." It is during this stage that the child imitates the communication of others. This coincides with the development of "intentionality." Intentionality is defined as the expression of an intention. The child has a goal in mind and uses communication to achieve that goal. For example, if the child wants Mom's attention, she may drop a toy from the highchair on purpose. Prior to this stage, the child dropped a toy accidentally during play and the parent retrieved and returned the toy. The 8-month-old now understands that if she drops a toy, mom will retrieve it. The intention is now there. She drops the toy on purpose (Owens, 2005). Recent research findings have demonstrated that children with ASD often have difficulty responding to their names during the latter half of the first year of life (Nadig, Ozonoff, Young, Rozqa, Sigman, & Rogers, 2007; Osterling, Dawson, & Munson, 2002; Werner, Dawson, Osterling & Dinno, 2000).

Language Development in Brief

A thumbnail sketch of early language development is provided as a quick reference. The reader should know that many books and texts are available that provide a full discussion of development. By one year of age, the child should be producing a large number of single-word utterances. This early vocabulary should include a large number of noun labels and also several verbs. By age 2, the child should be combining words into two-word utterances to express a number of semantic relations. That means the child may combine two words that express a number of different meaning dependent on the context in which the utterance is used. To illustrate, the child may say "doggie eat." This may mean the dog is eating its food. This might mean the dog is eating the child's food. It may mean that the dog is eating mom's favorite heels. Context is what is important here, not just the words used. By age three, the child should be combining three or more words into meaningful utterances. It is during this phase that words are combined based on the rules of syntax or grammar. The 3-year-old child in this stage of development would likely say "dog eat shoe" and one would not expect to hear "dog shoe eat." The emergence of syntactic or grammatical skills is not due to teaching from the environment but rather again references the prewiring of the human for language acquisition.

The Sounds of Language

Speech sounds develop in a sequence and some sounds are easier for the child to produce than others. What should be noted by parents is that a 3-year-old should be understood by those not familiar with them about 50% of the time. By age 4, this percentage climbs to 90% (Owens, 2005). This is important as speech sound errors can compromise the communication abilities of a child with ASD and need to be addressed. There are many anecdotal references in the literature to motor speech problems in children with ASD. Motor speech problems are described as difficulty sequencing and effectively producing consonant and vowels to produce understandable words. The diagnosis of motor speech concerns is challenging in this population and requires the services of a speech-language pathologist (SLP). The SLP is the professional who can assist in the assessment and treatment planning necessary to address this issue.

❖ Play and Social Skill Development ❖

There is a normal sequence for the development of play and social skills. Early on, play and social development are inextricably linked. Progress in one area directly impacts progress in the other. Foundational skills for play and social interaction result from the interactions of the infant and the caregivers.

Play falls into two dimensions, the symbolic and social. Each dimension will be discussed in terms of normal development and the problems with play demonstrated by children with ASD. Within the symbolic dimension, typically developing children engage in sensory exploration or manipulation which moves from repeated acts to variable acts and play combinations. This means that the child starts out banging and mouthing toys at about 6 months of age. However, this type of play shifts to more variable sensory play before the end of the first year. In the child with autism, sensory play may not shift to more varied play. The child may continue to bang and mouth objects well beyond the first birthday. The child may line up objects rather than physically manipulate them in a simple play script. The next phase of symbolic play is called functional play. This is defined as the conventional or common use of objects or toys. This means playing with toys in the way they were intended, driving toy cars rather than grouping them by color in precise lines. Following functional play, children move to pretend play. This is also called imaginative play. This may involve acting out roles and developing play scripts, such as cooking, or taking care of the toy animals as the veterinarian. Children with ASD often have the greatest difficulty in developing and demonstrating pretend play skills. Some children make little progress beyond sensory/manipulative play, hindering their transition through functional play to imaginative play. Others with ASD will develop rudimentary pretend play scripts. This means the child develops a highly restricted, inflexible script, playing the same way every time the cooking toys are presented. The child with ASD also may resist attempts by others to engage or alter their existing script.

With regard to the social dimension of play, the first phase is joint attention. This will be discussed extensively later in this chapter. There are several types of social play which include solitary play, parallel play, intersecting play, and interactive play. Solitary play is exactly what it sounds like, the child plays alone. Parallel play refers to children playing near one another with the same items but not crossing paths. During intersecting play, children occasionally will play within each others play space or with each others toys. The highest level of social play is interactive play. During this type of play, children share items, roles, and engage in variable play scripts with a variety of items. Children with ASD may become stuck in solitary play. This is understandable as solitary play allows the child to control the toys and control the outcomes. Occasionally, children with ASD may move into parallel or even intersecting play. Certainly interactive play is the most challenging for the child with ASD and successful interactive play may require extensive support from adults or even savvy peers.

Skills Supporting Play

Three developmental skills have been shown to be directly related to play and social skill development. These are joint reference, joint action, and turn-taking (Owens, 2005). Joint reference means that the infant and caregiver are both focused on the same object or event. Joint reference develops over the first 12 months of the child's life following a sequence of four phases. Phase One covers between 1 and 6 months of age and includes what is referred to as joint attention. For example, the dad might shake a rattle in front of the baby to get the baby's attention. Dad may then move the rattle near his own face to encourage eye contact. Phase Two is characterized by the infant demonstrating the intention to communicate and appears between 6 and 8 months of age. The infant may look at his mother, shift his gaze to a teddy bear and then back to his mother. In Phase Three, which emerges between 8 and 12 months, gestures and vocalizations are observed. The baby may reach for the bottle and vocalize babababa. In the final phase (Phase Four), at 12 months of age the child names a desired object in order to obtain it (Owens, 2005).

The development of joint action has long been noted to be vital to infant language learning and the development of the conventions of human communication. Joint action routines have been used in recent years as a mark of typical development and the lack of the development of joint action routines has been suggested to be a possible red flag or early indicator of the presence of an autism spectrum disorder. Joint action routines include game playing (peek-a-boo). During the first 6 months of life, game playing centers on child-caregiver interactions and is directly related to the development of play skills. During the second half of the first year, play shifts from interpersonal play to play with objects. Given that children with ASD have challenges relative to interpersonal play as well as play with objects, one can see why the development of joint action is of such interest to researchers and interventionists.

The reader probably can see that both joint reference and joint action are prerequisite skills for turn-taking. In the first year of life, the child and caregiver engage in what are called protoconversations. This pattern of reciprocal and alternating vocalizations may fail to develop if joint reference and action are lacking. Failure to engage in protoconversations is likely to result in a failure to develop true conversational skills, which are seen in the second year of life (Owens, 2005).

❖ Social Communication Development ❖

Wetherby and Prizant (1993) noted that children are able to communicate three intentions by their first birthday. These intentions are expressed first through gesture and then via words. These intentions include behavioral regulation, social interaction, and joint attention. Behavior regulation refers to the ways a child attempts to control the behavior of another person. This means that the child may request an action or object, first by pointing and later by using language. The child may try to regulate another by protesting, pushing an object or person away. Social interaction encompasses the way a child draws attention to him- or herself. This may include greeting (waving or saying bye-bye), calling, crying, or reaching to be picked up. Finally, joint attention references the ways a child would direct attention to an object or event in order to share that object or event with another.

Communication development and social development often are the first areas to show delays or disruptions in the child with ASD. The red flags that are seen in the first year of life relate to these areas. According to Wetherby et al. (2004), children who are later diagnosed with ASD may not respond to their names by 12 months of age. Additionally, they may not share attention to items and events with others. This lack of joint attention has been well documented over the past 20 years and research data indicate that this deficit is specific to ASD and not found in children who are demonstrating general developmental delays or a specific language deficit (Sigman, Mundy, Sherman, & Ungerer, 1986; Stone, Ousley, Yoder, Hogan, & Hepburn, 1997; Wetherby, Prizant, & Hutchinson, 1998; Wetherby & Prutting, 1984, Wetherby, Yonclas, & Bryan, 1989). Following 25 children with ASD over time, Siller and Sigman (2002) noted that the parents who synchronized their attention to their focus of their child's attention were able to increase their child's initiation of joint attention. Additionally, the best gains in language development occurred when the caregiver utterances were related to the child's attentional focus. This means the parent commented on what the child was doing and kept their language related to the toy or event at hand.

❖ Evidence-Based Interventions ❖

Just because a study is published, it does not mean the treatment will work for your child. If you are reading the published literature, you need to be a careful consumer of the literature. Many studies show promising results but that does not mean a particular treatment approach will benefit your child. When reading the research, ask some basic questions. The first question to ask is if the subjects of the study bear a significant resemblance to your child. For example, is your child in the age range of those in the study? Does your child have similar deficits in communication and social skills to the children in the study? If the answer to either question is no, then you should not pursue this article further. Even is the results are compelling, you cannot expect similar outcomes for your child unless your child is like the children in the study (O'Brien & Daggett, 2006).

If you find a study that includes subjects who are similar to your child, then you need to evaluate the findings in terms of expected outcomes. Are the changes from the intervention sustained for the long term? Is the cost of the intervention reasonable? Can your family incorporate this intervention into your daily life? If the answer is no to any of these questions, then perhaps this treatment is not for your child. With limited time, monetary, and emotional resources, families must be critical evaluators of the existing literature (O'Brien & Daggett, 2006).

Play Development

Guided participation, which follows assessment to determine the child's level of play skill development, is the intervention strategy used to address play skill acquisition. The adult must carefully observe and monitor the play of the child and peers. The adult then guides the children through play that supports interaction, creativity, communication, and imagination (Wolfberg & Schuler, 2006). Although the goal is for the children to play together without the intervention fo the adult, initially the adult plays a vital role in noting play initiations on the part of the child with ASD. If the child is not initiating play, the adult helps this occur. Once the child is initiating play, the adult scaffolds or supports the play to allow for script development. Just as a scaffold on a building is a temporary support, so is the role of the adult in the children's play. The adult should remove him- or herself from the play as skills develop. The adult has a significant role in guiding the social communication. This is another type of scaffolding where the adult supports the children as they respond to the communication of others, asking others to play, joining in with others (Wolfberg & Schuler, 2006). The growing body of research addressing play skill interventions can serve to improve outcomes for children with ASD (Lantz, Nelson & Loftin, 2004; Yang, Wolfberg, Wu, & Hwu, 2003; Zercher, Hunt, Schuler, & Webster, 2001).

❖ Language Development ❖

Language development interventions tend to fall into three categories, which include didactic behavioral approaches, naturalistic behavioral approaches, and developmental language approaches. Much information is available regarding specific strategies that fall under these headings. A brief summary is provided here to allow parents to find the intervention approach or approaches that will work for their individual child. No one treatment works for everyone.

Didactic Behavioral Approaches

The best known example of a didactic approach is discrete trial training (DTT) or the Lovaas approach. DTT relies on Skinner's model of operant conditioning as its foundation for language acquisition. It is an adult-directed treatment of massed trials and drills. The child does as directed by the adult and receives an extrinsic or token reward that is not necessarily related to the task at hand. This type of approach has a research base from single subject studies and some group research paradigms. The main strength of this type of treatment is that it is easily delivered via manuals and curricula. The weaknesses most often cited relate to the lack of naturalness in the learning environment, limited generalization of skills, and that it is not based in the current research data for communication development (Rogers, 2006).

Naturalistic Behavioral Approaches

Naturalistic approaches such as pivotal response training (PRT) also use Skinner's model of learning but in a more natural, child-centered context. The adult ensures that situations arise that elicit the child's interest and then follow the child's lead for more interaction. This type of treatment approach also has empirical support form single subject studies and a few group research studies. The strengths of naturalistic approaches are that they are in fact, naturalistic, using motivating activities in real-world settings. The limitations of naturalistic treatments are that there are no systematic manuals or curricula that allow for easy administration (Rogers, 2006)

Developmetal Language Approaches

Finally, approaches that are based in the developmental language arena include the social-communication, emotional regulation, transactional support (SCERTS) model (Prizant et al., 2000) and Floortime (Greenspan & Weider, 2000). This type of intervention is based on the current theory of language development, which is based on pragmatics or the social use of language. The research base for this approach is limited relative to other approaches, but several single-subject and group studies have been completed. Strengths of this approach include socially appropriate interaction in natural contexts with very motivating materials. The main criticism of these types of interventions is that they are based on the normal language development model and it is not yet known if children with ASD should follow this model. Additionally, these approaches are the most challenging to deliver because of the complexity of the targeted communicative behaviors (Rogers, 2006).

❖ Joint Attention ❖

A growing body of evidence that supports the hypothesis that joint attention, specifically the response to joint attention and the initiation of joint attention, is important to language development (Mundy et al., 1986; Sigman & Ruskin, 1999). Given that relationship one would expect to find evidence-based interventions that target both the response to and initiation of joint attention. Yoder and McDuffie (2006) described a continuum of interventions that range from naturalistic to discrete trial programs. Somewhere in between the two ends of this continuum lie interventions that seek to combine the best of both.

Naturalistic strategies are those that mirror the interactions that occur between parents and the child. Two examples of these strategies include responsive training (RT; Mahoney & McDonald, 2003) and Floortime (Greenspan & Wieder, 2000). Both focus on the relationship between the child and therapist, both avoid adult-directed activities and punishment. A perceived weakness of naturalistic approaches may be the lack of specific attention to joint attention. DTT interventions are adult-directed, involve token reinforcement and do not specifically address joint attention (Yoder & McDuffie, 2006).

Two types of interventions, transactional approaches and combined approaches, include both naturalistic strategies and the practice strategies associated with discrete-trial training (DTT). An example of a transactional approach is the Social-Communication, Emotional Regulation, Transactional Support model or SCERTS (Prizant et al., 2000). In the SCERTS model, the child initiates the activity and only after the initiation are prompts used. This allows the adult to follow the child's lead (naturalistic) and then provide prompts for increased interaction as needed. The goal of this type of approach is to avoid one of the potential pitfalls of DTT, which is prompt dependence. Combined approaches include principles from transactional approaches and DTT. An example comes from the work of Whalen and Screibman (2003). Following compliance training (DTT), the child is then provided with instruction in responding to joint attention cues.

What makes the transactional and combined approaches attractive is that they seem to use the best of both worlds with regard to effective treatment approaches. It is essential for parents to recognize that the ends of the intervention continuum (naturalistic approach, DTT) may not adequately address two of the essential deficits in ASD, joint attention and the need for step-by-step compliance training. It is important to note that all intervention is best served by being administered in the child's natural environment. The National Research Council (NRC) noted in 2001 that children with ASD need functional and meaningful opportunities to learn in their natural environments in order to facilitate generalization (Wetherby & Woods, 2008). Family support and involvement is essential to the success of any treatment program.

Ultimately, early intervention is the key to the best outcomes. Along with early intervention comes the need for early identification. Professionals are challenged to administer effective screening and surveillance protocols to try and ensure that children with ASD are identified early and evidence-based interventions are administered. Several screening tools are available to the general medical practitioner and can be readily administered to the child or parent during a routine well-baby check. The Modified Checklist for Autism in Toddlers (M-CHAT) (Robins & Dumont-Mathieu, 2006; Robins, Fein, Barton, & Green, 2001) is a parent report tool while the Pervasive Developmental Disorders Screening Test (PDDST) (Siegel, 1996; Siegel & Hayer, 1999) is administered to the child. Both of these tools are considered Level 1 or population screeners. Level 2 or focused screeners include the Systematic Observation of Red Flags (SORF) (Wetherby & Woods, 2002), Social Communication Questionnaire (SCQ) (Rutter, Bailey, Lord, & Berument, 2003). These tools are administered if there are concerns raised by a Level 1 screener or physician referral.

❖ Pitfalls in Play ❖

Most children have too many toys. Most have too much stuff. One of the pitfalls parents should avoid is purchasing too many toys. For a child on the autism spectrum, one puzzle, one ball, one train, one package of animals may be enough toys to have out at one time. Nothing is more disheartening that to see a child wander amid dozens and dozens of toys, playing with none, unable to attend to any of the playthings. In this instance, less is more. In addition, many toys lack a cognitive challenge. If the toy works on batteries or a simple remote control, it may not provide a learning opportunity, and with children with ASD, all play should be a learning opportunity. For the young child, look for toys that require fine motor skills as well as simple problem-solving skills. This combination can provide the cognitive challenge necessary to foster ongoing cognitive growth and development.

Another pitfall parents should avoid is excessive exposure to some cartoon and video game characters. A review of the literature did not reveal any studies that would support this recommendation.

This is experience speaking. Children with ASD can become very involved with cartoon characters, to the exclusion of many other types of activities. Certainly, some cartoons have learning opportunities inherent in them and these may provide a positive contribution to development. Others may have a focus on good versus evil, or superheroes. Superheroes may provide many children with a positive lesson in good versus evil. However, many superhero characters overcome wrongdoing with physical force. For children who have limited or disrupted social and coping skills, physical force should not be a viable solution to problems. Why? Because the child with ASD often cannot determine that physical force is not appropriate. I would submit that physical force has no place in the problem-solving repertoire of any child, but certainly not those who may not understand the difference between fantasy and reality.

Along the same lines, video gaming may not be a viable play strategy for many children with ASD. Problems that might arise from some games include limited cognitive challenge, and socially unacceptable problem-solving strategies (physical force, intimidation). Parents are cautioned to recognize that video and computer-based games should first and foremost provide a positive learning opportunity as well as some degree of cognitive challenge. As the child with ASD gets older, these other types of games, cartoons, videos, and the like may be introduced. But, for younger children on the spectrum, parents are encouraged to carefully review and consider all media their child uses on a regular basis.

❖ What I Believe ❖

I believe that parents need to be actively involved in all therapeutic interventions their child is receiving. No data exist to support the idea that professionals serving a child a few hours a day or week, without parental participation and involvement will cause any significant, long-term impact on the development of children with ASD. Parents should read about intervention strategies and determine which approach or approaches they find manageable for their family.

I believe that the development of joint attention is essential to later improvements in skills in children with ASD and should be a major focus in treatment. I believe that combined treatment approaches that focus on skill acquisition in naturalistic settings provide the best outcomes for most kids with ASD, at least in regard to generalization of learning. I believe play skills often are overlooked and essential to later cognitive and language development. Play with your child. Engage him or her in play. Demonstrate appropriate play with developmentally appropriate toys.

I believe that the less a child plays with specifically branded toys, the better. Avoid characters and focus on the toy itself, not the picture on it. I have found this helps kids develop greater flexibility in play skills and in choosing toys to play with at school or in day care. Speech-language pathology graduate students have been challenged for years to do treatment with a box of facial tissues. You want to stretch your play skills? Try being creative in play with tissues! Seriously, spend your hard earned dollars on sturdy toys that will teach your child new and meaningful skills.

CHAPTER 7

All in the Family

Ultimately, autism is a disorder that changes over time. It is a dynamic problem that may manifest in certain behaviors at one age that disappear later. There is progress, and the occasional regression. The cause of regression is not known and the mechanism of regression is not fully understood. Some children regress when not enrolled in school or other intervention services. Others show regression of skills when they are ill. There are certainly ups and downs associated with the disorder itself and in the rearing of the child with autism. Children with autism can, with appropriate support and intervention, become adaptable people with a variety of skills and abilities. There is no one description that can adequately and correctly describe the course of this disorder in the life of the child. The following insights are offered from my professional experiences over the past 20 years. Real parents of real children who have autism or Asperger syndrome also offer their insights to assist you as you begin or continue this journey.

❖ Objects in the Mirror Are Closer ❖ Than They Appear

Do not be surprised to look at yourself as the parent and see similarities between you and your child. Maybe you like things to be a certain way and become frustrated when things are not that way. If that is the case, then spend some time thinking about how you feel when things do not go your way. Think about how you start to feel when unplanned events are thrust upon you. How do you respond when your plans are changed without notice? Is it any wonder that a child who lives very much in the here and now might have a meltdown when something unexpected happens? If you can get in touch with your own feelings about changes, you may be able to relate more to your child's feelings.

The whole "mirror" thing also relates to the future. It is closer than you think. The transition to preschool is just around the corner and so is elementary school and puberty, and adulthood. Now, I do not mean to suggest that you not live right in the moment with your child. But you must live with an eye to the future. Plan ahead. Be prepared.

❖ What Families Have Taught Me ❖

Aileen and Chad

Aileen and Chad brought their 18-month-old son to me seeking information relative to the significant regression he had just experienced. Jackson, now 8 years of age and moderately to severely autistic, has given his parents life lessons. They graciously shared these lessons with me. I recall the day Chad said, "You are not afraid of the meltdowns, are you?" I asked him if he was afraid of them. He replied that he and Aileen were both afraid of the meltdowns and as a result avoided them at all costs. I asked how they avoided them and he noted that they backed off from challenging Jackson as soon as he began to vocalize in protest. This meant he was never allowed to become frustrated enough to cry or scream. What is concerning about this approach is that, although it did avoid triggers, it did not allow for the development of alternative strategies. By focusing on avoiding conflict and not what triggered the conflict, the parents were not facilitating their son's development. They realized that the meltdown was not the end of the world and that, although often embarrassing and attention getting, they had to engage the potential meltdowns head on and deal with what triggered them as well as develop alternative responses in their son.

Kristal and Brian

Kristal and Brian are the parents of a son with Asperger syndrome (AS) and a daughter with high functioning autism (HFA). Brian also has characteristics consistent with AS, but no formal diagnosis. What this couple taught me was the power of patience and flexibility. Kristal in particular is the most patient of people. She has to be as she is surrounded by persons on the spectrum or at least very near it. She takes each day as it comes. She lives in the moment and encourages that in her children. This keeps her kids from fearing what will happen next. She lives the credo that what will happen will happen, and worrying won't change it. As a testament to this philosophy, Kristal invited her husband's nephew to come live with her family. This young man was 17 years of age, undiagnosed with either AS or HFA, who was failing high school, unemployed, and probably being abused in his own home. Kristal integrated him into her existing home schedule, got him on track in school, and working with Brian.

Matt and Serena

No matter how many times professionals told Matt and Serena that their children's behaviors were not acceptable, they continued to make excuses. They said that their daughter was too tired to work in therapy and that she should have her reward anyway. They stated that their son spit because he had autism and someone must have done something to him to trigger the spitting. Their motivation for the excuses was not known to me but I can hypothesize that they simply were unable to come to terms with the fact that both their children were impaired. They seemed to persist in the belief that autism was both an explanation and an excuse for problem behaviors. Yes, ASD explains why a child hits or spits but it does not give a child license to behave badly. Both children had effective communication systems available to them. They were able to get their needs met so these aberrant behaviors were not noted when they were expressing wants and needs. They hit and spit when they wanted to avoid activities in school and therapy, and their parents enabled them. The lesson here is not a warm and fuzzy one.

Patricia and the Summer of Driving

Patricia had been told by her child's 5th grade teacher that her son needed to learn to be more flexible. He was a stickler for following his daily schedule without variation. Schedules need to vary so Patricia set out to help him be more flexible. She asked him every day during the summer what he wanted to do that day. His favorite activities included the library and the pool. Mom packed him up every day with whatever was needed for the preferred activity. Instead of driving directly to the pool, she ran errands, did other activities, but they always ended up at the chosen activity. By the end of the summer, he would get in the car and say "Are you going to mess with me again today, Mom?" He reportedly entered middle school much better able to deal with unexpected events and changes to his schedule.

Charlotte and BIG Points

Charlotte found that her son Jake would work for points. He had done this for years with great success. However, she noted a sudden change in his enthusiasm for points. She decided to up the points value associated with tasks. She also increased the points needed to earn rewards. For example, what was once worth 10 points went up to 100 points. Instead of needing 50 points a week to earn rewards, he now needed 500. This worked quite well and when her son was faced with really challenging new tasks, the point values doubled or tripled as needed.

Pam and the Chocolate Closet

Pam is the parent who introduced me to dietary intervention. I saw firsthand what this treatment can do for a child with food sensitivities. Her son, Ethan, was on a gluten/casein free diet. Pam liked chocolate a great deal and found she needed it in times of high stress. She felt she could not have candy and such in the house as Ethan might accidentally find it and eat it. She also realized she needed that available for her own needs. We had seen what happened when he was off diet and it was frightening, so Pam kept a shoe box full of chocolate snacks in her bedroom closet. She spoke of a particularly trying day when Ethan refused to eat his chicken and supplements. Once he finally ate, Pam went into her room, closed herself in the closet and ate a candy bar. What Pam taught me is that parents are mere mortals who need candy sometimes!

The Blue Divided Plate

John and Marilyn called me after their 24-year-old daughter stopped eating. It seems that Annie had eaten off a blue divided plastic plate for the past 23 years, or for as long as they could remember.

One morning, to their horror, they found the plate had not survived the dishwasher. It had melted beyond recognition. What I learned from John and Marilyn that, although it seemed a good idea to allow Annie to eat off the same plate every day for every meal, in reality they had handicapped her. She had been led to believe that food always came on a blue divided plate. She had desired a predictable routine. The plate kept her calm. However, John and Marilyn did her no favors in leading her to believe that things would always be the way she wanted them to be. The lesson we can take from this is not to set our kids up with expectations that cannot be met.

Scott's Collectibles

Scott and his son share a great interest in stock car racing. Scott has a number of collectibles related to this interest. His son asked if he could play with them and Scott explained that they are valuable and that he plans to leave them to his son when he passes away. His son looked right at him and, with a great big smile, anticipating the great play opportunity, asked his dad when he was planning on dying. Initially taken aback as Scott is new to the world of ASD, he realized quickly that his son meant no harm and was really just trying to figure out when he could play. Scott realized that life is lived now and that his son lives in this moment. They play with all the collectibles and have a blast sharing their love of racing.

Marilyn and Maggie

Maggie liked everything to stay the same. Marilyn loved change. One day Marilyn rearranged the living room furniture while Maggie was at school. Maggie came home and was upset by the changes. Marilyn assured Maggie that all the things she was used to and loved were still in the room, just in a different place. Marilyn decided to rearrange things in her home about once a month, again while Maggie was in school. Sometimes she just moved things around on shelves and tables. Other times she moved furniture as well. She did not ever rearrange Maggie's room. One day Maggie asked if she and her mom could rearrange her bedroom. Her mom agreed of course and they moved things around. Two months later, Maggie asked if they could paint her room a whole new color.

Logan the Wanderer

Logan was only 4 years old when he wandered away the first time. Imagine the parent's terror at realizing their son with moderate autism was missing. He was found about two miles from his home in the mountains of Virginia. Luckily, he was unharmed, but the parents were not. They were riddled with guilt. How could they have been so careless? They were not really careless. They just underestimated their son. He wanted to go for a walk and he did. Whether he was following a butterfly (his favorite thing at that time) or something else, they never determined. What they did determine is that they needed a way to keep him safe. They worked closely with the local sheriff and got Logan an ankle monitor that communicates with a receiver unit at the sheriff's office. He wandered away a couple more times, but he never got further than the long family driveway before the family got a call from the sheriff.

Jacob the ASD Advocate

When Jacob turned 10, he asked his mother why he had trouble making friends and why he went for group therapy at the local university. She told him with honesty and clarity that he had something called Asperger syndrome. She explained that the AS made it hard for him to make friends sometimes because he would only talk about what he cared about and not what others wanted to discuss. She reminded him that he was not always a good loser at games and that others did not always want to play with him. She explained that he was not mentally retarded, but that some school work like language arts was hard for him while science was an area where he excelled. He asked if he caught AS from somewhere, and she assured him he did not. He asked if he could tell others about AS and she assured him he could. He got a ribbon lapel pin and a blue rubber bracelet. He answered questions when his peers asked him about his pin and bracelet. He also informed total strangers at the mall. He became his own best advocate.

Jordan, the Walking Encyclopedia

Jordan's mother Chris learned early on what Asperger syndrome was and how it might impact her son. She determined that he would not become a habitual TV watcher or video gamer. She and her children lived in a rural area with no cable TV. She outfitted her home with books. Lots and lots of books! She had a set of encyclopedias. Jordan read everything. He played outside in the gorgeous mountain community in which he lived. He worked in the family garden. He studied stars with his telescope as there was no light pollution where they lived. He studied art and pottery at the local collective. He went to bluegrass jams and square danced. He filled his days with learning, knowledge, and nature. He was perhaps the most well-rounded, calmest, most engaging young man it was ever my pleasure to meet.

❖ Real Information from Real Parents ❖

In response to the questions "What are the best lessons you have learned in raising your child with ASD? What do you want other parents to know?"

This is my favorite quote as a parent of a child with autism.

"For most of the ordinary people—parents and other relatives of children with autism—the heroism lies in the bits and pieces that few people ever see. It is in the poetry of our everyday lives, the special foods we cook for our picky eaters, the challenges we surmount to take our children to the dentist or a physician, the hugs we give even when our children do not hug back . . .

Change is forced upon us, and we embrace it, often without realizing how much we are doing."
—Unstrange Minds, *by Roy Richard Grinker (2007)*

Here are my tips:

❖ *Keep up the good work (you are a hero every day)*

❖ *Remain optimistic*

❖ *Examine the evidence (get your child the therapy he/she needs and deserves right away, especially those backed by evidence)*

❖ *Go with your gut (you know your child best, so use your instincts)*

❖ *Surround yourself with support*

❖ *Take breaks (you need to take care of yourself, too)*

❖ *Dream big!*

Hugh is my inspiration. Let your child inspire you. Don't despair. This may not at all be the direction you expected your life to take, or that of your child. But while some doors have been closed, others have been opened. I know it may be hard, but look for those open doors and take a nice walk through!

AS

I suppose one of the most important lessons (and best) would be learning how to think like my son. When I take the time to anticipate, review, and look at situations through his eyes, his perspective, we both enjoy a better life. I have learned to love the 'view' that my son has of the world and often wish—I could share his vision with those less understanding, flexible or compassionate.

To other parents: Enjoy the journey, cherish and celebrate each small success, every day. Love your child, embrace their gifts and walk with them through the looking glass and into the world.

CH

TO LOVE: I have learned more about love than I could ever imagine, I have learned to love unconditionally, without expecting anything in return.

TO UNDERSTAND: I have learned understanding, because there are reasons for the way my son reacts to situations and why, and it's up to me to understand, and help him.

TO HAVE PATIENCE: Not only for my son, but for all the idiots in the world that don't understand him, or AS!

TO BE A TEACHER: Because it's up to us as parents to educate the world about our children.

And lastly, I have learned that ASPERGER SYNDROME is not a diagnosis or a disability, but rather, it's a gift that my son was blessed with that makes him unique, special, and who he is.

VA

I think the biggest and best lesson of all is that at first Cameron's mother and I were devastated to learn that our baby boy had this disorder. I feel more and more every day that we were chosen to be his parents by God himself. We don't know why but that's how we feel. He must have seen something in us that maybe we didn't see in ourselves. Cameron has a large support system and that is definitely a plus. Also Cameron is a very smart child. He problem solves, he has learned to deal with over stimulating situations well, and he is very mischievous as any other 7-year-old would be. Another good lesson learned is that Cameron to us is like any other child. He laughs when he thinks something is funny, cries when sad, pouts when he don't get his way, sometimes gets grumpy when sleepy. With the exception of his ASD, Cameron is as normal as most. Cameron knows what he wants and he usually figures out how to get it. He is becoming more sociable every day. Just this morning, he said to a friend "HELLO BENNY!" and was totally un-prompted but very appropriate. My message to all you parents out there who have a child with ASD—love them, work with them, and most of all thank God in Heaven for your precious Angel as we have!

SM

My three children with autism have taught me to live in the moment. There are so many books and people advocating for "mindful" living, living and seeing the beauty of the present. However, most of us continue to make plans way into the future and rush through the here and now by over committing ourselves and not prioritizing our obligations. To give you an example, my family was in the backyard one spring day. I of course was cleaning, picking up toys and debris. I noticed my oldest, Catherine, standing still and just staring into the sky. After observing her for a few minutes, I walked over to her and asked her what she was looking at. She pointed up and said "tree." I looked up. It was a beautiful day, no clouds, bright and sunny, with a slight breeze.

The leaves on the tree reflected the sunlight and swayed with the gentle breeze. She watched this smiling. I thought to myself, "When was the last I just stopped and looked at a tree, admiring its beauty, watching the curves of the leaves, and the lines of the bark?" So I stood with her and watched the tree, enjoying its beauty, in complete awe of God's gifts, Catherine and the tree.

JM

The biggest lesson I have learned being a parent with a child on the spectrum is that I am her STRONGEST advocate. It is essential for parents to educate themselves about ASD and to KNOW their rights and resources. The more I learn, the stronger my voice is for my little girl.

RB

There are many things I have learned living in a household where I am the only one who is not on the spectrum. The biggest and best lesson would have to be to have plenty of patience. Have patience and be flexible. With many things in life you have to learn by trial and error. If something is not working for your family, try it other ways until you find the right balance. If at some point that way no longer works, find yet another way. You have to follow the clues of the person or people on the spectrum to see how the things you do affect them. No matter if they are a newly diagnosed 3-year-old or a full grown adult you have to try your best to help guide them through life and above all else love them no matter what. What I want other parents to know about their child is that no one else will ever know your child like YOU do. No one else will ever have that unconditional love that you have for your child. You can take your child to all the specialists, therapies, and classes you want and chances are you will meet some well intended people. At the end of the day, though, you and you alone are the one who will be there for your child. You know all their quirks, habits, fears, and joys. YOU are the one who has to follow your heart and make the final choices for your child. They might not always be the "right" choices but you have to hope and pray they are the "best" ones for your child, your family, and even you.

KE

Asperger Syndrome or "High-Functioning Autism" and the Broad Spectrum Disorders which include ADD/ADHD, Sensory Integration Dysfunction, Concept Imagery Dysfunction (Hyperlexia), Dyslexia, Generalized Anxiety Disorder, are a part of the fastest growing developmental disability in this country. Just knowing what those terms meant, along with a list of symptoms that I could identify, would have given me much incentive to investigate and develop better physical/mental coping mechanisms that would have kept me from isolating myself from my peers and developing a whole host of other problems (i.e. Social Anxiety Disorder, severe lack of pragmatic social skills, and the inability to recognize non-verbal language cues, which makes up for 93% of all human communication). I, as well as many others, have come to view the disorder as being defined by multiple sensitivities which include the internal as well as the external. I happen to believe that there could possibly be joint causes responsible for the development of the disorder. A catalyst (genetic predisposition), and an inducer (childhood vaccinations) working in conjunction with one another. I base this belief on my own personal experience. As an infant, I had a seizure from a DPT vaccination at the age of 2 months. Many years later, my third cousin, who is 15 years my junior, suffered from a seizure like the one I experienced immediately after a vaccination. Both of us developed Asperger syndrome, she being more severely affected than I, with many other health problems as well. As far as we are aware after much research of our family history, we are the only ones to have developed the disorder so far. What that says to me is that these vaccines may be safe for some people, but can and may cause extreme adverse effects in others. At this time, there is no way currently to determine who may be most at risk. A primary focus needs to be on early intervention for the identification of the disorder, which is paramount to the success of treatment and ultimately will determine the quality of life for many suffers. Had this been the case for me, I would have benefited greatly from it. Instead I had to try to cope and adapt to the world around me as best I could, which in many ways operates in a backwards manner to the mindset of an Autistic. Much of my own success came from my sheer will and determination not to let what had happened cripple me to the extent that it would destroy my life and future. I am currently beginning my senior year in college where I am double major-

ing in history and philosophy. I have done well and gained a lot of ground, but it hasn't been easy. Although I have developed many friendships over the years, the more in-depth and intimate interpersonal relationships many Autistics desire to achieve in our personal lives continues to be a struggle. It is something I am constantly working on. Anxiety and doubt tend to be a constant in my life even at this point. To some extent, they always may be there. A lot of the pain, suffering, loneliness, and trauma that I, and many others like me, experienced growing up could have been drastically reduced, or avoided altogether if I had been given the early intervention I so desperately needed. Socialization difficulties stemming from AS are at the roots of all AS evils. Teach those who have AS/HFA to "small talk" with their peers and elders. An excellent source of information on this topic is discussed in great length in the book, The Fine Art of Small Talk, *by Debra Fine. If these main issues are addressed: socialization, reading comprehension (hyperlexia, dyslexia, etc.), and assessment of anxiety by targeting its root causes, the quality of life for the millions of those suffering from the disorder in the next generation could be drastically improved to the degree that many will ultimately lead the normal lives they so desperately desire, and deserve. They can be spared of the upbringing that I had to endure.*

CS

❖ What I Believe ❖

I believe that parents often learn best from other parents. Find other parents of children with ASD and talk to them. Ask them what works, what does not. Hold each others' hands. Hold each others' hearts. Be honest with each other. Be honest with yourselves. Take a break. Get away. You need to rejuvenate your body, mind, and spirit, so you can continue to raise your wonderful, unusual, strange, smart, challenging, odd, captivating, and often trying, but always precious, child.

References

Adams, L. (2007). *Autism and Asperger syndrome: Busting the myths.* San Diego, CA: Plural.

Adams, L., & Conn, S. (1997) Nutrition and its relationship to autism. *Focus on Autism and Other Developmental Disabilities, 12*(1), 53–58.

Adams, L., Gouvousis, A., VanLue, M., & Waldron, C. (2004). Social story intervention: Improving communication skills in a child with Autism Spectrum Disorder. *Focus on Autism and Other Developmental Disabilities, 19*(2), 87–94.

Aspy, R., & Grossman, B. (2007). *The Ziggurat model: A framework for designing interventions for individuals with autism and Asperger syndrome.* Shawnee Mission, KS: Autism Asperger Publishing.

Bach, J. (2005). Infections and autoimmune diseases. *Journal of Autoimmunity, 25,* 74–80.

Baron-Cohen, S., & Swettenham, J. (1997). Theory of mind in autism: Its relationship to executive function and central coherence. In D. Cohen & F. Volkmar (Eds.), *Handbook of autism and pervasive developmental disorders* (2nd ed., pp. 880–893). Oxford, UK: John Wiley and Sons.

Baron-Cohen, S., Tager-Flusberg, H., & Cohen, D. (1993). *Understanding other minds: Perspective from autism.* Oxford, UK: Oxford University Press.

Benayed, R., Gharani, N., Rossman, I., Mancuso, V., Lazar, G., Kamdar, S., et al. (2005). Support for the homeobox transcription factor gene ENGRAILED 2 as an autism spectrum disorder susceptibility locus. *American Journal of Human Genetics, 77,* 851–868.

Bernard-Opitz, V., Sriram, N., & Nakhoda-Sapuan, S. (2001). Enhancing social problem solving in children with autism and normal children through computer-assisted instruction. *Journal of Autism and Developmental Disorders, 31*(4), 377–384.

Booth, R., Charlton, R., Hughes, C., & Happe, F. (2003). Disentangling weak coherence and executive dysfunction: Planning drawing in autism and attention-deficit/hyperactivity disorder. In U. Frith & E. Hill (Eds.), *Autism: Mind and brain* (pp. 211–223). New York: Oxford University Press.

Burnett, C., Mundy, P., Myer, J. A., Sutton, S., Vaughan, A., & Charak, D. (2005). Weak central coherence and its relations to theory of mind and anxiety in autism. *Journal of Autism and Developmental Disorders*, *35*(1), 63–73.

Campbell, D., Sutcliffe, J., Ebert, P., Militerni, R., Bravaccio, C., Trillo, S., et al. (2006). A genetic variant that disrupts MET transcription is associated with autism. *Proceedings of the National Academy of Sciences, 103*(45), 16834–16839.

Case-Smith, J., & Bryan, T. (1999). The effects of occupational therapy with sensory integration emphasis on preschool-age children with autism. *American Journal of Occupational Therapy, 53*, 489–497.

Charlop-Christy, M., Carpenter, M., Le Blanc, L., & Kellet, K. (2002). Using the Picture Exchange Communication System (PECS) with children with autism: Assessment of PECS acquisition, speech, social communicative behavior, and problem behavior. *Journal of Applied Behavior Analysis, 35*, 213–231.

Croen, L., Najjar, D., Ray, G., Lotspeich, L., & Bernal, P. (2006). A comparison of health care utilization and costs of children with and without autism spectrum disorders in a large group-model health plan. *Pediatrics, 118*(4), 1203–1211.

Dawson, G., & Watling, R. (2000). Interventions to facilitate auditory, visual and motor integration in autism: A review of the evidence. *Journal of Autism and Developmental Disorders, 30*, 415–421.

Dunlap, G., dePerczel, M., Clarke, S., Wilson, D., Wright, S. White, R., & Gomez, A. (1994). Choice making to promote adaptive behavior for students with emotional and behavioral challenges. *Journal of Applied Behavior Analysis, 27*, 505–518.

Durand, C., Betancur,C., Boeckers, T., Bockmann, J., Chaste, P., Fauchereau, F., et al. (2007). Mutations in the gene encoding the synaptic scaffolding protein SHANK3 are associated with autism spectrum disorders. *National Genetics, 39*(1), 25–27.

Ernsperger, L., & Stegen-Hanson, T. (2004). *Just take a bite: Easy, effective answers to food aversions and eating challenges.* Arlington, TX: Future Horizons.

Frith, U. (1989). *Autism: Explaining the enigma.* Oxford, UK: Basil Blackstock.

Foster-Johnson, L., Ferro, J., & Dunlap, G. (1994). Preferred curricular activities and reduced problem behavior in students with intellectual disabilities. *Journal of Applied Behavior Analysis, 27*, 493–504.

Goldberg, E. (2001). *The executive brain: Frontal lobes and the civilized mind.* New York: Oxford.

Greenspan, S., & Wieder, S. (2000). Developmental approach to difficulties in relating and communicating in autism spectrum disorders and related syndromes. In A. Wetherby & B. Prizant (Eds.), *Autism spectrum disorders: A transactional developmental perspective* (Vol. 9, pp. 279–303). Baltimore: Paul H. Brookes.

Hart, B., & Risly, T. (1995). *Meaningful differences in the everyday experiences of young American children.* Baltimore: Paul H. Brookes.

Herskowitz, V. (2008). Using technology to learn and grow: Computer-based intervention for individuals with autism. *Autism Advocate, 52*(3), 18–22.

Hieneman, M., Childs, K., & Sergay, J. (2006). *Parenting with positive behavioral support: A practical guide to resolving your child's difficult behavior.* Baltimore: Paul H. Brookes.

Horner, R. Carr, E., Strain, P., Todd, A., & Reed, H. (2002). Problem behavior interventions for young children with autism: A research synthesis. *Journal of Autism and Developmental Disorders, 32*(5), 423–446.

Horvath, K., Papadimitriou, J. Rabsztyn, A., Drachenberg, C., & Tilden, J. (1998). Gastrointestinal abnormalities in children with autistic disorder. *Journal of Pediatrics, 135,* 559–563.

Hughes, C. (2001). Executive dysfunction in autism: Its nature and implications for everyday problems experienced by individual with autism. In J. A. Burack & T. Chairman (Eds.), *The development of autism: Perspectives from theory and research.* (pp. 255–275). Mahwah, NJ: Lawrence Erlbaum Associates.

Janzen, J. (2003). *Understanding the nature of autism: A guide to the autism spectrum disorders.* San Antonio, TX: PsychCorp.

Jepson, B. (2007). *Changing the course of autism: A scientific approach to treating your autistic child.* Boulder, CO: Sentient.

Kanner, L. (1943). Autistic disturbances of affective content. *Nervous Child, 2,* 217–250.

Kellner, M. (2003). *Anger management skills for parents of young adolescents.* Champaign, IL: Research Press.

Klinger, L., & Dawson, G. (1992). Facilitating early social and communication development in children with autism. In S. F. Warren & J. Reichle (Eds.), *Volume 1: Causes and effects in communication and language intervention* (pp. 157–186). Baltimore: Paul H. Brookes.

Koegel, L., & Koegel, R. (2006). *Pivotal response treatments for autism.* Baltimore: Paul H. Brookes.

Lantz, J., Nelson, J., & Loftin, R. (2004). Guiding children with autism in play: Applying the integrated play group model in school settings. *Exceptional Children, 37*(2), 8–14.

Linderman, T., & Stewart, K. (1998). Sensory-integrative based occupational therapy and functional outcomes in young children with pervasive developmental disorders: A single-subject design. *American Journal of Occupational Therapy, 53,* 207–213.

Maestro, S., Muratori, F., Cavallaro, M., Pei, F., Stern, D. Golse, B., et al. (2001). Early behavioral development in autistic children: The first two years of life through home movies. *Psychopathology, 34*(3), 147–152.

Magiati, I., & Howlin, P. (2003). A pilot evaluation study of the Picture Exchange Communication System for children with Autistic Spectrum

Disorder. *Autism: the International Journal of Research and Practice,* 7, 297–320.

Mahoney, G., & McDonald, J. (2003). *Responsive teaching: Parent-mediated developmental intervention.* Cleveland, OH: Case Western Reserve University.

Millward, C., Ferriter, M., Calver, S., & Connell-Jones, G. (2004). Gluten-and casein-free diets for autism spectrum disorders [Review]. Cochrane Development, Psychosocial and Learning Problems Group. *Cochrane Database of Systematic Reviews, 2.*

Moore, M., & Calvert, S. (2000). Vocabulary acquisition for children with autism: Teacher or computer instruction. *Journal of Autism and Developmental Disorders, 30,* 359–362.

Mundy, P., Sigman, M., Ungerer, J. & Sherman, T. (1986). Defining social deficits in autism: The contribution pf non-verbal communication measures. *Journal of Child Psychology and Psychiatry, 27,* 657–669.

Myles, B., & Simpson, R. (2001). Understanding the hidden curriculum: An essential social skill for children and youth with Asperger syndrome. *Intervention in School and Clinic, 36,* 279–286.

Myles, B., & Simpson, R. (2003). *Asperger syndrome: A guide for educators and parents* (2nd ed.). Austin, TX: Pro-Ed.

Nadig, A., Ozonoff, S., Young, G., Rozqa, A., Sigman, M., & Rogers, S. (2007). A prospective study of response to name in infants at risk for autism. *Archives of Pediatric and Adolescent Medicine, 161*(4), 378–383.

National Research Council. (2001). *Educating children with autism.* Washington, DC: National Academy Press.

Neihus, R., & Lord, C. (2006). Early medical history of children with autism spectrum disorders. *Journal of Developmental Behavioral Pediatrics, 27*(2), 120–127.

O'Brien, M,. & Daggett, J. (2006). *Beyond the autism diagnosis: A professional's guide to helping families.* Baltimore: Paul H. Brookes.

Osterling, J., Dawson, G., & Munson, J (2002). Early recognition of 1-year old infants with autism spectrum disorder versus mental retardation. *Development and Psychopathology, 14*(2), 239–251.

Owens, R. (2005). *Language development: An introduction* (6th ed.). Boston: Allyn & Bacon.

Ozonoff, S., Dawson, G., & McPartland, J. (2002). *A parent's guide to Asperger syndrome and high-functioning autism: How to meet the challenges and help your child thrive.* New York: Guilford Press.

Pellicano, E., Maybery, M., & Durkin, K. (2005). Central coherence in typically developing preschoolers: Does it cohere and is it related to mindreading and executive control? *Journal of Child Psychology and Psychiatry, 46*(5), 533–547.

Prizant, B., Wetherby, A., & Rydell, P. (2000). Communication intervention issues for children with autism spectrum disorders. In A. Wetherby & B. Prizant (Eds.), *Autism spectrum disorders: A transactional developmental perspective* (pp. 193–224). Baltimore: Paul H. Brookes.

Randall, P., & Parker, J. (1999). *Supporting the families of children with autism.* Chichester, UK: John Wiley & Sons.

Ray, T., King, L., & Grandin, T. (1988). The effectiveness of self-initiated vestibular stimulation in producing speech sounds in an autistic child. *Occupational Therapy Journal of Research, 8,* 186–190.

Reichelt, K. Knivsberg, A., Nodland, M., & Lind, G. (1994). Nature and consequences hyperpeptiduria and bovine casomorphines found in autistic syndromes. *Developmental Brain Dysfunction, 7,* 71–85.

Reilly, C., Nelson, D., & Bundy, A. (1984). Sensorimotor versus fine motor activities in eliciting vocalization in autistic children. *Occupational Therapy Journal of Research, 3,* 199–212.

Robins, D., & Dumont-Mathieu, T. (2006). Early screening for autism spectrum disorders: Update on the Modified Checklist for Autism in Toddlers and other measures. *Journal of Developmental and Behavioral Pediatrics, 27,* S111–S119.

Robins, D., Fein, D., Barton, M., & Green, J. (2001). The Modified Checklist for Autism in Toddlers: An initial study investigating the early detection of autism and pervasive developmental disorders. *Journal of Autism and Developmental Disorders, 31,* 131–144.

Rogers, S. (2006). Evidence-based interventions for language development in young children with autism. In T. Charman & W. Stone (Eds.), *Social and communication development in autism spectrum disorders: Early identification, diagnosis, and intervention* (pp. 143–179). New York: Guilford Press.

Rogers, S., & Ozonoff, S. (2005). What do we know about sensory dysfunction in autism? A critical review of the empirical evidence. *Journal of Child Psychology and Psychiatry, 46,* 1255–1268.

Rosemond, J. (2008, July). Do your child a favor-never tolerate tantrums. *Coastal Family,* Savannah, GA.

Rubin, L. (2006). *Using superheroes in counseling and play therapy.* New York: Springer.

Rutter, M. (2000). Genetic studies of autism: From the 1970s to the millennium. *Journal of Abnormal Psychology, 28,* 3–14.

Rutter, M., Bailey, A., Lord, C., & Berument, S. (2003). *Social Communication Questionnaire.* Los Angeles: Western Psychological Services.

Shattock, P., Kennedy, A., Rowell, F., & Berney, T. (1990). Role of neuropeptides in autism and their relationships with classical neurotransmitters. *Brain Dysfunction, 3,* 328–345.

Sherer, M., & Schriebman, L. (2005). Individual behavioral profiles and predictors of treatment effectiveness for children with autism. *Journal of Consulting and Clinical Psychology*, *73*, 525–539.

Siegel, B. (1996). *Pervasive Developmental Disorders Screening Test (PDDST)*. Unpublished manuscript.

Siegel, B. (2008). *Getting the best for your child with autism. An expert's guide to treatment.* New York: Guilford Press.

Siegel, B., & Hayer, C. (1999, April). *Detection of autism in the 2nd and 3rd year: The Pervasive Developmental Disorders Screening Test (PDDST).* Paper presented at the Society for Research in Child Development, Albuquerque, NM.

Sigman, M., Mundy, P., Sherman, T., & Ungerer, J. (1986). Social interactions of autistic, mentally retarded, and normal children and their caregivers. *Journal of Child Psychology and Psychiatry*, *27*, 647–656.

Sigman, M., & Ruskin, E. (1999). Continuity and change in social competence of children with autism, Down syndrome, and developmental delays. *Monographs of the Society for Research in Child Development*, *64*(1).

Siller, M., & Sigman, M. (2002). The behaviors of parents of children with autism predict the subsequent development of their children's communication. *Journal of Autism and Developmental Disorders*, *32*, 77–89.

Simpson, R. (2005). Evidence-based practices and students with autism spectrum disorders. *Focus on Autism and Other Developmental Disabilities*, *20*(3), 140–149.

Smith, T., & Wick, J. (2008). Controversial treatments. In K. Chawarska, A. Klin & F. Volkmar (Eds.), *Autism spectrum disorders in infants and toddlers* (pp. 243–273). New York: Guilford Press.

Stone, W., Ousley, O., Yoder, P., Hogan, K., & Hepburn, S. (1997). Nonverbal communication in 2- and 3-year old children with autism. *Journal of Autism and Developmental Disabilities*, *27*, 677–696.

Sutcliffe, J., Delahanty, R., Prasad, H., McCauley, J., Han, Q., Jiang, L., et al. (2005). Allelic heterogeneity at the serotonin transporter locus (SLC6A4) confers susceptibility to autism and rigid-compulsive behaviors. *American Journal of Human Genetics*, *77*, 265–279.

Sweeten, T., Posey, D., & McDougle, C. (2004). Brief report: autistic disorder in three children with cytomegalovirus infection. *Journal of Autism and Developmental Disabilities*, *34*(5), 583–586.

Volkmar, F., Westphal, A., Gupta, A., & Wiesner, L. (2008). Medical issues. In K. Chawarska, A. Klin, & F. Volkmar (Eds.), *Autism spectrum disorders in infants and toddlers: Diagnosis, assessment and treatment* (pp. 274–299). New York: Guilford Press.

Wassink, T., Brzustowicz, L., Bartlett, C., & Szatmari, P. (2004) The search for autism disease genes. *Mental Retardation Developmental Disabilities Research Review*, *10*(4), 272–283.

Watson, L., Lord, C., Schaffer, B., & Schopler, E. (1989). *Teaching sponta-neous communication to autistic and developmentally handicapped children.* New York: Irvington.

Werner, E., Dawson, G., Osterling, J., & Dinno, N. (2000). Brief report: Recognition of autism spectrum disorder before one year of age: A ret-rospective study based on home videotapes. *Journal of Autism and Developmental Disorders, 30*(2), 157–162.

Wetherby, A., & Prizant, B. (1993). *Communication and Symbolic Behav-ior Scales-Normed Edition.* Baltimore: Paul H. Brookes.

Wetherby, A., Prizant, B., & Hutchinson, T. (1998). Communicative, social-affective, and symbolic profiles of young children with autism and per-vasive developmental disorder. *American Journal of Speech-Language Pathology, 7,* 79–91.

Wetherby, A., & Prutting, C. (1984). Profiles of communicative and cognitive-social abilities in autistic children. *Journal of Speech and Hearing Research, 27,* 364–377.

Wetherby, A., & Woods, J. (2002). *Systematic observation of red flags for autism spectrum disorders in young children.* Unpublished manual, Florida State University, Tallahassee.

Wetherby, A., & Woods, J. (2008). Developmental approaches to treatment. In K. Chawarska, A. Klin, & Volkmar, F. (Eds.), *Autism spectrum disor-ders in infants and toddlers: Diagnosis, assessment and treatment* (pp. 170–206). New York: Guilford Press.

Wetherby, A., Woods, J., Allen., Cleary, J., Dickenson, H., & Lord, C. (2004). Early indicators of autism spectrum disorders in the second year of life. *Journal of Autism and Developmental Disorders, 34,* 473–493.

Wetherby, A., Yonclas, D., & Bryan, A. (1989). Communication profiles of handicapped preschool children: Implication for early identification. *Journal of Speech and Hearing Disorders, 54,* 148–158.

Whalen, C. & Schreibman, L. (2003). Joint attention training for children with autism using behavior modification procedures. *Journal of Child Psychology and Allied Disciplines, 44*(3), 456–468.

Wheeler, M. (2004). *Toilet training for individuals with autism and related disorders.* Arlington, TX: Future Horizons.

Willis, C. (2006). *Teaching young children with autism spectrum disor-der.* Beltsville, MD: Gryphon House.

Wolfberg, P., & Schuler, A. (2006). Promoting social reciprocity and symbolic representation in children with autism spectrum disorders: Designing quality peer play interventions. In T. Charman & W. Stone (Eds.), *Social and communication development in autism spectrum disorders: Early identification, diagnosis, and intervention* (pp. 180–218). New York: Guilford Press.

Yang, T., Wolfberg, P., Wu, S., & Hwu, P. (2003). Supporting children with autism spectrum in peer play at home and school: Piloting the integrated play groups model in Taiwan. *Autism: The International Journal of Research and Practice, 7*(4), 437–453.

Yoder, P., & McDuffie, A. (2006). Treatment of responding to and initiating joint attention. In T. Charman & W. Stone (Eds.), *Social and communication development in autism spectrum disorders: Early identification, diagnosis, and intervention* (pp. 117–142). New York: Guilford Press.

Zercher, C., Hunt, P., Schuler, A., & Webster, J. (2001). Increasing joint attention, play and language through peer supported play. *Autism: The International Journal of Research and Practice, 5*, 374–398.

APPENDIX A

Resources for Parents

Overcoming Autism: Finding the Answers, Strategies, and Hope That Can Transform a Child's Life by Lynn Koegel and Claire LaZebnik: A compassionate book for parents.

A Parent's Guide to Asperger Syndrome and High Functioning Autism by Sally Ozonoff, Geraldine Dawson, and James McPartland: A parent-focused book for successful child rearing.

Autism and Asperger Syndrome: Busting the Myths by Lynn Adams: Accessible information regarding definitions, assessment procedures, and treatment strategies.

Changing the Course of Autism by Bryan Jepson: A medical professional's journey through a maze of research.

Just Take a Bite by Lori Ernsperger and Tania Stegen-Hanson: Commonsense approach to food aversion and problem eating.

Parenting with Positive Behavior Support by Meme Hieneman, Karen Childs, and Jane Sergay: Practical information for supporting your child with challenging behavior.

Positive Discipline for Single Parents by Jane Nelsen, Cheryl Erwin, and Carol Dezler: General information for the single parent.

Staying in Control by Millicent Kellner: An excellent resource for parents of teens.

The Autism Encyclopedia by John Neisworth and Pamela Wolfe: Definitions and explanations for the myriad terms associated with autism.

Toilet Training for Individuals with Autism and Related Disorders by Maria Wheeler: Step-by-step guide for the development of independent toilet training.

Understanding the Nature of Autism by Jan Janzen: A text for professionals that is extremely accessible for parents.

Getting the Best for Your Child with Autism: An Expert's Guide to Treatment by Bryna Siegel: A guide written with humor and excellent information.

❖ Organizations ❖

Parent Support

Autism Society of America
7910 Woodmont Ave
Suite 300
Bethesda, Maryland 20814-3067
Tel: 1.800.3AUTISM (328.8476)
Web site: http://www.autism-society.org

ASA, the nation's leading grassroots autism organization, exists to improve the lives of all affected by autism by increasing public awareness about the day-to-day issues faced by people on the spectrum, advocating for appropriate services for individuals across the lifespan, and providing the latest information regarding treatment, education, research and advocacy, founded in 1965 by Dr. Bernard Rimland, Dr. Ruth Sullivan and many other parents of children with autism.

National Autism Association
1330 W. Schatz Lane
Nixa, Missouri 65714
Tel: 1.877.NAA.AUTISM (622.2884)
Web site: http://www.nationalautismassociation.org

The mission of the National Autism Association is to educate and empower families affected by autism and other neurological disorders, while advocating on behalf of those who cannot fight for their own rights. NAA takes the stance that autism is not a lifelong incurable genetic disorder but one that is biomedically definable and treatable. It works to raise public and professional awareness of environmental toxins as causative factors in neurological damage that often results in an autism or related diagnosis. It supports funding efforts toward this end through appropriate research for finding a cure for the neurological damage from which so many affected by autism suffer.

Autism Speaks
Offices in New York, NY, Princeton, NJ, and Los Angeles, CA
Web site: http://www.autismspeaks.org

At Autism Speaks, the goal is to change the future for all who struggle with autism spectrum disorders. Autism Speaks is dedicated to funding global biomedical research into the causes, prevention, treatments, and cure for autism; to raising public awareness about autism and its effects on individuals, families, and society; and to bringing hope to all who deal with the hardships of this disorder. It is committed to raising the funds necessary to support these goals.

Research Information

Autism Research Institute
Tel: 1.866.366.3361
Web site: http://www.autism.com

The Autism Research Institute (ARI), a non-profit organization, was established in 1967. For more than 40 years, ARI has devoted its work to conducting research, and to disseminating the results of research, on the triggers of autism and on methods of diagnosing and treating autism. It provides research-based information to parents and professionals around the world.

Organization for Autism Research
2111 Wilson Blvd.
Suite 600
Arlington, VA 22201
Tel: 1.703.351.5031
Web site: http://www.researchautism.org

The Organization for Autism Research (OAR) was created in December 2001. Led by the parents and grandparents of children and adults on the autism spectrum, OAR set out to use applied science to answer questions that parents, families, individuals with autism, teachers and caregivers confront daily. No other autism organization has this singular focus.

National Alliance for Autism Research
99 Wall Street
Research Park
Princeton, NJ 08540
Tel: 1.888.777.NAAR (6227)
Web site: http://www.naar.org

The National Alliance for Autism Research (NAAR) was the first national nonprofit organization in the country dedicated to funding and accelerating biomedical research exclusively for autism spectrum disorders.

Government Resources

The Center for Disease Control and Prevention (CDC)
Autism Information Center
Web site: http://www.cdc.gov/ncddd/autism/

The CDC serves as the national focus for developing and applying disease prevention and control, environmental health, and health promotion and health education activities designed to improve the health of people in the United States.

The National Institute of Mental Health (NIMH)
6001 Executive Blvd, Room 8184, MSC 9663
Bethesda, Maryland 20892-9663
Tel: 1.866.615.6464
Web site: http://www.nimh.nih.gov/healthinformation/
autismmenu.cfm

The National Institute of Mental Health (NIMH) is the largest scientific organization in the world dedicated to research focused on the understanding, treatment, and prevention of mental disorders and the promotion of mental health.

Education Support

The Office of Special Education and Rehabilitative Services (OSERS)
U.S. Department of Education
400 Maryland Avenue, SW
Washington, DC 20202-7100
Tel: 1.202.245.7468
Web site: http://www.ed.gov/about/offices/list/osers/index.html

The Office of Special Education and Rehabilitative Services (OSERS) is committed to improving results and outcomes for people with disabilities of all ages. OSERS provides a wide array of supports to parents and individuals, school districts and states in three main areas: special education, vocational rehabilitation and research.

Council for Exceptional Children
1110 North Glebe Road
Suite 300
Arlington, VA 22201
Tel: 1.703.620.3660
Web site: http://www.cec.sped.org

The Council for Exceptional Children works to improve and influence public policy affecting children with exceptionalities, those with disabilities and/or gifts and talents, their parents, and the professionals who work with them, at all levels of government.

Wrightslaw-Special Education
Web site: http://www.wrightslaw.com/info/autism.index.htm

Parents, educators, advocates, and attorneys come to Wrightslaw for accurate, reliable information about special education law, education law, and advocacy for children with disabilities.

Professional Associations

American Speech-Language-Hearing Association
2200 Research Blvd.
Rockville, Maryland 20850-3289

Tel: 1.301.296.5700
Web site; http://www.asha.org

The American Speech-Language-Hearing Association is the professional, scientific, and credentialing association for more than 130,000 members and affiliates who are speech-language pathologists, audiologists, and speech, language, and hearing scientists in the United States and internationally. Its focus is on promoting effective human communication.

American Occupational Therapy Association, Inc.
4720 Montgomery Lane
PO Box 31220
Bethesda, Maryland 20824-1220
Tel: 1.301.652.2682
Web site: http://www.aota.org

The American Occupational Therapy Association advances the quality, availability, use, and support of occupational therapy through standard-setting, advocacy, education, and research on behalf of its members and the public.

American Physical Therapy Association
1111 N. Fairfax Street
Alexandria, VA 22314-1488
Tel: 1.703.684.APTA (2782)
Web site: http://www.apta.org

The mission of the American Physical Therapy Association (APTA), the principal membership organization representing and promoting the profession of physical therapy, is to further the profession's role in the prevention, diagnosis, and treatment of movement dysfunctions and the enhancement of the physical health and functional abilities of members of the public.

Association for Behavioral Analysis
219 South Park Street
Kalamazoo, MI 49001
Tel: 1.269.492.9310
Web site: http://www.abainternational.org

The Association for Behavior Analysis International is a nonprofit professional membership organization with the mission to contribute to the well-being of society by developing, enhancing, and supporting the growth and vitality of the science of behavior analysis through research, education, and practice.

American Psychiatric Association
1000 Wilson Blvd.
Suite 1825
Arlington, VA 22209-3901
Tel: 1.703.907.7300
Web site: http://www.psych.org

The American Psychiatric Association is devoted to psychiatry and its impact on those suffering from mental illnesses.

American Psychological Association
750 First Street NE
Washington, DC 20002-4242
Tel: 1.800.374.2721
Web site: http://www.apa.org

The mission of the American Psychological Association is to advance creation, communication and application of psychological knowledge to benefit society and improve people's lives.

APPENDIX B

Basic Vocabulary for Parents

Achievement testing: refers to the tools that assess reading, math, writing, and other academic skills.

Adaptive skills: skills needed to function effectively in typical everyday situations.

Age appropriate: can refer to chronological age (actual age) or developmental age (estimate based on developmental level)

Antecedent: what comes before a response. In problem behavior, it refers to what triggers the behavior.

Applied behavior analysis: Based on the principles of operant conditioning. Requires the observation of behavior, analysis of the function of the behavior, and application of intervention to alter the behavior. Also known as ABA, DTT, or Lovaas approach, although these are not actually interchangeable terms.

Asperger syndrome: related to autism, may be a variation or separate disorder. Characterized by social impairments but in the absence of cognitive and language deficits. Significant difficulty understanding and demonstrating social rules governing communication which are also known as pragmatics. Acutely aware of social deficits. Sometimes not diagnosed until late elementary school or labeled early on as PDD-NOS.

Assessment: a process, not an event, meaning that information is gathered over time from a variety of sources in a variety of contexts for the purpose of evaluation. Can lead to diagnosis and is used to monitor progress in a treatment protocol.

Augmentative/Alternative Communication: strategies used to facilitate or replace verbal communication. May include paper picture-based systems, voice output devices, computer-assisted technology, and sign/gestural systems. Also known as AAC.

Autism: a developmental disorder characterized by communication and social interaction difficulties as well as cognitive differences/ challenges. Unusual sensory responses, difficulty with transitions, adherence to routine; repetitive movements/actions. Symptoms can be present from birth or can become prominent between 1½ to 3 years of age.

Autism Spectrum Disorder: Although not a formal diagnostic category, the term refers to a collection of developmental disorders that include autism, Asperger syndrome, pervasive developmental disorders-not otherwise specified (PDD-NOS), Rett syndrome, and childhood disintegrative disorder. Sometimes used to characterize all of the above except autism.

Behavior: Not just bad things people do, behavior is anything that a living organism does, good or bad. Behavior can be classified as related to communication, social, motor, etc.

Behavior analyst: trained professional who assesses behavior and develops and implements intervention based on the assessment.

Cognition: thinking, attention, memory, problem solving abilities. What IQ tests purport to measure. Refers to what the brain does in terms of taking in information, processing it, storing it, and responding.

Communication: Formulating, transmitting, and processing information using speech and language skills. Includes the use of speech and language for the exchange of information and in the social context.

Developmental delay: delay in the development of skills at the same approximate age as peers. Developmental milestones are the age markers used to measure the degree of delay.

Diagnosis: collection of information through tests, observations, and so on to determine an appropriate label to help with treatment planning. In educational settings, a nonmedical label used in some schools to allow for effective treatment planning. In medical settings, a process used to develop effective treatment planning

Discrete trial training: an approach developed by Lovaas. Tasks are broken down into steps and the child is trained on each step through repeated practice or trials. Also referred to as the Lovaas approach and sometimes ABA model, but these are not really interchangeable terms.

DSM-IV: the manual used by professionals for diagnoses of disorders and diseases. (Acronym for *Diagnostic and Statistical Manual-4th edition.*)

Early intervention: intervention provided before the age of 3 years and shown to improve long-term outcomes. Early identification and diagnosis results in intervention services that attempt to diminish developmental delays.

Echolalia: repetition of another's words, phrases, or sentences. Also includes replication of the person's intonation, inflection, and/ or accent. Can be immediate (right after a person speaks) or delayed (by several minutes or more). Can be mitigated, meaning other than the alteration of perhaps one word, the utterance is identical.

Etiology: the cause of any disease or disorder. There is no single cause for autism.

Evidence-based: referring to treatment strategies that have been subjected to examination in an empirical study. Treatment claims should be supported by data.

FAPE: free appropriate public education. Key word is appropriate in that schools must provide services to meet the unique needs of each child.

Floortime: common name given to approach developed by Greenspan and Wieder. Also known as DIR (Developmental, Individual-Difference, Relationship-based) model. Often referred to as Greenspan model.

Functional: means that the skill or task being taught or trained serves a function in the everyday life of the person.

Generalization: taking skills learned in one context or environment and demonstrating them in another different context or environment. Very challenging for persons with ASD.

Gluten-free/casein-free diet: dietary intervention that removes all wheat and dairy proteins in addition to other grains. Limited empirical data available, but large body of anecdotal support from parents who have tried this. Very challenging to effectively implement due to processing of most foods. Not the same as an organic diet or the Feingold diet.

Greenspan model: Also known as Floortime or DIR.

Hand over hand: the technique where the adult puts his or her hands over those of the child to guide the child through an action or movement/task.

Head circumference: measurement around the skull that follows a predictable pattern. Children with ASD can show increased head circumference in infancy and toddler years.

High-functioning autism (HFA): when a child has autism and a measured IQ above 85. Not a formal diagnostic category in DSM-IV. Some debate as to whether it is actually Asperger syndrome. Anecdotally, some report that those with HFA do not appear aware of differences whereas those with Asperger syndrome do.

IDEA (Individuals with Disabilities Education Act): the federal law governing special education services to children from birth to 21 years.

IEP: stands for Individualized Education Program, which is a document mandated by federal law for all students, aged 3 to 21, who are receiving special education services in public schools. Parent participation is required during the development of the program.

IFSP: stands for Individualized Family Service Plan, which is a document mandated by federal law for children receiving specialized services between the ages of birth and 3 years.

Inclusion: placing the child in the general education classroom with typically developing peers.

Intervention: another word for treatment or therapy. A set of procedures and objectives meant to alter an area of development.

Joint attention/joint action: focus of child and adult on each other, the same item or same activity. Very important skill to be developed in child with ASD. Often lacking in the child with ASD in the second half of the first year.

Language: set of rules that govern how sounds are combined into words, words are placed into classes, and words are organized into phrases and sentences. Also rules for how two people interact in the context of a conversation. Also relates to the way individuals create stories or narratives.

Receptive language—what you understand or comprehend
Expressive language—what you say or produce

LEA (Local Education Agency): the agency that serves the county or district school system.

LRE (least restrictive environment): school placement that provides best learning outcomes with the least amount of restriction. May be the general education classroom, but may not be. There is no single type of LRE.

Lovaas approach: also referred to as DTT.

Mental retardation: deficit in cognitive, intellectual, and adaptive skills. IQ score of less than 70 is considered to be indicative of mental retardation. Can co-occur with ASD.

Motor skills: fall into two categories of fine and gross motor skills. Fine motor refers to skills requiring more precise coordination of smaller muscles such as writing, drawing, dressing, and so on. Gross motor skills are those using larger muscle groups such as walking or running, catching, throwing.

NCLB (No Child Left Behind Act): 2001 legislation that focuses on accountability of schools with emphasis on the development of reading.

Neurologist: medical professional who specializes in the structure and function of the central nervous system including the spinal cord, brainstem, cerebellum, and both cerebral hemispheres.

Occupational therapy/therapist: therapy focused on the development of fine motor skills including dressing, writing, drawing, and feeding. Therapist holds a minimum of a bachelor's degree and passes a national examination to obtain certification. Most states require licensure.

Pervasive developmental disorder: a developmental disorder that impacts or pervades the acquisition of cognition, communication, and social and motor skills. In the DSM-IV, an umbrella term that encompasses autism, Asperger syndrome, Rett syndrome, childhood disintegrative disorder,, and pervasive developmental disorder-not otherwise specified (PDD-NOS).

Pervasive developmental disorder-not otherwise specified: PDD-NOS is used when child does not meet full criteria for other disorder under PDD umbrella. Might be labeled as high functioning autism or Asperger syndrome later.

Physical therapy/therapist: therapy focused on the development of gross motor skills including walking, running, catching, throwing, and so on. Therapist holds a minimum of a bachelor's degree and holds a license to practice in the state.

Positive behavioral support: preventing behavior concerns by analyzing situations, triggers, and functions of behavior. Proactive approach to dealing with problem behavior.

Psychiatrist: medical professional with training in the area of mental health assessment and treatment. Can order diagnostic testing and prescribe medications.

Psychological testing: the assessment tools used to measure cognitive and adaptive skills including memory, problem solving, and adaptability. Traditional tools use verbal language in the administration. Nonverbal measures are also available.

Psychologist: professional who studies human behavior. Typically requires a graduate degree, certification, and licensure. Specialty areas include child, clinical, educational, developmental, and organizational. Generally does not prescribe medications.

Respite care: support for parents provided in the home to allow for time away from the child with special needs.

Savant: exceptional skill or ability, not taught, inherent in the person. Not every person with ASD has a savant skill.

Self-injurious behavior: scratching, biting, head banging demonstrated by some with severe ASD.

Sensory: referring to the senses and the processing of information through the senses. Senses include sight, hearing, touch, taste, smell. Also includes body in space awareness or proprioception.

Social skills: the ability to interact with others in conversations and groups in a variety of contexts. Skills include eye contact, physical proximity, turn-taking, topic introduction, and maintenance. Includes the ability to rapidly read a situation and respond accordingly.

Social stories: a trademarked name for a specific type of intervention strategy for social skill instruction. Variations include social scripts, social dialogues.

Speech: the coordination of lips, teeth and tongue for the production of sounds that are combined to form words.

Speech-language pathology/pathologist: therapy focused on the development of speech (sound production) and language (words, phrases, sentences), and communication. Includes stuttering articulation disorders, and language delay/disorder as well as the use of augmentative/alternative communication (AAC). Requires a master's degree, national examination for national certification, state licensure in most states.

Stereotypic behaviors: self-stimulating behaviors including hand flapping, rocking, twirling, humming, etc. Done by the child for the child.

TEACCH: model and curriculum for teaching and education children with ASD.

Team: multidisciplinary, interdisciplinary, transdisciplinary models of groups of professionals for the assessment and treatment of children with special needs.

Therapy: another word for treatment or intervention. A set of procedures and objectives meant to alter an area of development.

Transitions: movements from one activity to another, from one place to another, from one setting to another. Often very challenging for the person to stop one activity to move to the next and to move from one place to the next. Also refers to the movement from settings such as when a child moves from a preschool to elementary school.

Treatment: another word for therapy or intervention. A set of procedures and objectives meant to alter an area of development.

Visual clutter: the "stuff" in our environment that may interfere with necessary visual support strategies.

Visual schedule: a system for representing the order of steps, tasks, or events in a visual fashion. Objects, photos, pictures, and print symbols are used to denote the order in which things need to happen. The adult equivalent is a day planner or personal digital assistant. Schedules can aid in transitions by reducing anxiety about what will happen next.

Visual support strategies: refers to the collection of visual representations that facilitate and support the person with ASD. Schedules, calendars, cue cards, stories, and AAC are all types of visual strategies. Some supports aid in with the input of information like schedules, whereas others support output like AAC systems.

Index

A

Adams, Lynn, 101
American Occupational Therapy
    Association, 106
American Physical Therapy
    Association, 106
American Psychiatric Association,
    107
American Psychological
    Association, 107
American Speech-Language-
    Hearing Association,
    105–106
Ankle monitor, 85
Applied behavior analysis (ABA),
    109
ASD (autism spectrum disorder)
    causes, theoretical, 5–7
    and central coherence, 7
    characteristics, 7–8
    and chemicals, 6–7
    definition, 110
    and environment, 6–7
    executive function overview, 7
    explanation/not excuse, 21
    genetics, 5–6
    and metabolic challenges, 6, 29
    myths, 2–3
    and ToM (theory of mind), 7
    and toxins, 6–7
    truths, 2
    and viral infection, 6
Asperger syndrome, definition, 4,
    109

Asperger syndrome and autism,
        high functioning
    definition, 4–5
Association for Behavioral Analysis,
    106–107
Attention, joint, 74–76, 77–78, 112
Autism and Asperger Syndrome
        (Adams, Lynn), 101
Autism definition, 3–4, 110
The Autism Encyclopedia
        (Neisworth & Wolfe), 101
Autism Research Institute, 103
Autism Society of America, 102
Autism Speaks, 103

B

Behavior challenges management
    alternative behavior provision,
        21
    and anger, 20–21
    ASD: explanation/not excuse,
        21, 82
    behavior functional analysis,
        15–16
    channeling from undesired to
        desired activity, 18–19
    choice provision, 14–17
    and communication needs,
        12–17
    coping strategies provision, 21
    cues to support/prompt, 19
    and demeanor, parental, 19
    demeanor importance, 21–22
    direction giving, 19